A-LEVEL YEAR 2 SOCIOLOGY FOR

UNIT 3A (Globalisation & the Digital Social World)

SOCIOLOGY 3A STUDY GUIDE

Published independently by Tinderspark Press
© Jonathan Rowe 2021
www.psychologywizard.net
www.philosophydungeon.weebly.com

Visit the **Sociology Robot** YouTube channel

CONTENTS

ABOUT THIS BOOK

This book offers advice for teachers and students approaching OCR A-Level Sociology, **Paper 3 Section A (Globalisation & the Digital Social World)**.

The Study Guides for **Paper 3B (Options in debates in contemporary society)** will follow.

Paper 3 Section A

This covers a third of **Paper 3** in OCR Sociology. There are 3 questions worth 35 marks out of the 105 marks for the entire paper. It should take candidates 45 minutes to complete.

3A (Globalisation & the Digital Social World) reintroduces some foundational concepts that candidates have met earlier in their Sociology A-Level: the idea of **Global Culture** and **aspects of Identity** along with **Marxism** and **Feminism** from **1A** and also **Postmodernism** that was introduced in **1B**.

Perspectives

This Study Guide reintroduces candidates to 3 important sociological Perspectives: **Marxism**, **Feminism** and **Postmodernism**. These were introduced in the Study Guides for Paper 1 but are reiterated here in a new context.

Up until now, Functionalism has appeared as the opposing view to the Conflict Theories (Marxism and Feminism) but it does not appear in this Section. Candidates can bring up Functionalist ideas to evaluate Marxism, Feminism and Postmodernism and to help with this I mention them on occasions (however rare such arguments might be in academic Sociology).

The New Right Perspective does not feature in this section; neither does Interactionism, although Labeling Theory would make a good alternative explanation for some of the topics covered here.

Studies

Sociological 'studies' (for A-Level purposes) are often papers published in academic journals, but are sometimes magazine articles, pamphlets produced by charities or activists or popular books.

Where texts are particularly famous or influential, I offer their names, but candidates are not expected to know the names of studies in the exam. All the studies referenced in this Study Guide are brought together at the end in a revision aid (p72).

GLOBALISATION & THE DIGITAL SOCIAL WORLD: CONTENT

What's this topic about?

This introduces you to the main theories in Sociology, in particular the concept of GLOBALISATION and how it influences us. You will also learn about the DIGITAL REVOLUTION (p27) and its IMPACT on society (p38).

This should help you answer some important questions:

- What is globalisation: is it good or bad and (important question) for whom in particular? Is it a powerful force in society or a declining one?

- What are digital forms of communication? How are they different from traditional communication? Who benefits from this new technology and who loses out?

- What are the impacts of digital communication on society? Are our lives enriched or impoverished? Should we be concerned or excited by the prospect of a digitally connected world?

Globalisation

In **1A: Socialisation, Culture & Identity**, you learned about **Global Culture**. Globalisation is the process that is bringing this Global Culture into being – and it is having other effects too.

Globalisation is often described as the world getting smaller. Not physically smaller, of course, but smaller in the sense of being more connected, with faster travel, better communication and stronger economic links. Television brings us news stories from parts of the world that were mysterious to most people in Europe and America only 50 years ago. Air travel means ordinary people can go to far away places to work or holiday. Migration means that people who used to consider each other 'foreigners' are now neighbours. And of course, the World Wide Web makes communication instantaneous and opens up new knowledge and experiences to ordinary people.

One consequence of this has been the appearance of **Trans-National Corporations** (**TNCs**). These companies started off based in one country but have grown to be worldwide business with more wealth than some small countries. Examples of TNCs include the car company **Toyota** (from Japan), the food company **Nestlé** (from Switzerland) and the fast-food chain **McDonald's** (from the USA) as well as the **'Tech Giants'** like **Facebook** and **Google**.

Alongside the TNCs are other groups with a worldwide reach: **Non-Government Organisations** (**NGOs**) which aren't businesses looking for a profit. These include **Greenpeace**, the **World Wildlife Fund (WWF)** and **Oxfam**. Many of these organisations have the wealth (from donations) and prestige to influence world governments.

CHAPTER ONE – DEFINITIONS OF GLOBALISATION

Globalisation can be understood in different ways and interpreted optimistically (as an exciting new era of opportunity) or pessimistically (as a threat to things that people have valued for generations or a way for the rich and the powerful to exploit everyone on the planet).

Positive Views of Globalisation

The positive view of Globalisation can be summed up in the word '**opportunity**.'

For most of human history, people lived in tribes, cut off from each other, figuring things out for themselves through trial and error, making slow progress and viewing outsiders with suspicion. Globalisation is the end of all that. Now there's one big human tribe emerging with everyone talking to everyone else, learning and progressing.

For some people this is an opportunity to experience new things: to travel, enjoy other cultures and lifestyles, taste new food and listen to new music. It's an opportunity to educate yourself and learn. It's also about political opportunities, for countries that used to squabble over borders to come together and solve problems that would be too big for them alone. Finally, there are economic opportunities, to sell goods to new markets, find new customers and workers, buy new products and offer people services who used to lack access to them. These services can be recreational or lifesaving: everything from video games to vaccines.

Positive views of Globalisation often (but not always) come from the **Postmodernist** Perspective.

Negative Views of Globalisation

Negative views of Globalisation are split between the fear of **homogeneity** and the fear of **exploitation**.

Homogeneity means "everything being the same" and Globalisation threatens to swamp the world with versions of the same cultural products: everyone in jeans and T-shirts, drinking Coke, eating Big Macs, listening to the same R&B music, watching the same TV shows and big budget movies; ultimately, everyone speaking the same language. Quirky local differences and deeply significant religious and cultural traditions all risk being washed away. This means "the world getting smaller" in a less attractive sense: the world getting less interesting and less varied.

Exploitation means the poorer people being oppressed. Critics of Globalisation fear that the only people to benefit from those wonderful opportunities will be the super-rich. Globalisation means that these elite businesspeople no longer have to be restrained by the laws of the country they live in. They are above the law now and can set about making themselves even richer without anything to hold them back. This view of Globalisation focuses on how people in the poorest countries work for a pittance while their resources and environment are stripped away and their own governments can no longer protect them.

Concerns about exploitation often come from the Conflict Perspectives (**Marxism** and **Feminism**).

Problems with Defining Globalisation

Anything with the word 'global' (meaning 'all over the world') in it is going to be huge and complex – perhaps too huge and complex for humans to take it in and sum it up, which is why we have problems defining Globalisation.

Let us use a definition from the sociologist **Anthony Giddens (1990)**:

"[Globalisation is] *the intensification of worldwide social relations which link distant localities in such a way that local happenings are shaped by events occurring many miles away and* vice versa"

This definition includes key features such as: (1) **worldwide social relations**, not just between countries but between continents; (2) **links between distant localities and local happenings**; (3) the *'vice versa'* meaning that globalisation works in two directions, influence coming from far away but also your own influence being felt far away.

But what do we mean by these *'worldwide social relations'*? There are three main definitions.

Anthony Giddens (photo: Eirik Helland Urke)

Cultural Globalisation

This is the way in which cultures that used to be distinct and separated from each other by oceans and deserts and mountain ranges are now encountering each other, blending together and influencing each other. In past centuries, a few travellers, merchants, missionaries and explorers went off to encounter foreign peoples and brought back tales (often exaggerated or garbled) of their culture. Now, thanks to cheap travel, worldwide communication and migration, ordinary people encounter each other's cultures as a part of everyday life.

Sociologists have three responses to this:

Cultural homogeneity: Some sociologists claim this is leading to a **homogenous Global Culture** where everyone acts and things the same, wearing the same fashions, listening to the same music, watching the same films and eating the same food. Marxists are particularly worried that this homogenous Global Culture is really the Capitalist **Consumer Culture** of the USA and Europe, with its inequalities and ruling class ideologies; it is a type of **cultural imperialism**, dominating other societies. **Feminists** are concerned that this culture will not respect the rights of women, exporting sexism all around the world. However, cultural homogeneity might be a *good* thing if it replaces cultural practices that are racist or homophobic or misogynistic (anti-women).

Cultural Defence: Other sociologists point out that communities react to Globalisation by emphasising their own cultural distinctiveness: it becomes *more* important for them, not less, that they teach their children their traditional language and religion and pass on their customs. This can be attractive – such as the struggle to maintain languages like Welsh and Gaelic as Global Culture becomes increasingly anglophone (English-speaking). However, it also leads to **religious fundamentalism**, which (sometimes violently) rejects Global Culture in favour of a hyper-intense version of local religious traditions.

Cultural Defence is covered in more detail in **Chapter 3**, p49.

Cultural Hybridity: Finally, there is the possibility that individuals or groups 'mix & match' the aspects of Global Culture, creating their own **Hybrid Culture** (for a group) or **Hybrid Identity** (for a person). This is a popular view with **Postmodernists**, who claim we construct our identities from the images and ideas available to us in the Media. This choice can be empowering, but there is growing concern about **cultural appropriation**, which is when people from a privileged culture (such as White Americans) adopt aspects of less-privileged cultures in a disrespectful or ignorant way.

US soldier with captured ISIS flag

AO2 ILLUSTRATION: ISLAMIC STATE

Islamic State (also known as **ISIS** or **ISIL**) originated in 1999 but it became famous (or infamous) in 2014 when it captured a big area of territory in Iraq and later Syria. ISIS was identified as a terrorist organisation by the United Nations; it carried out massacres of civilians and the enslavement or execution of prisoners.

ISIS is a religious fundamentalist group and could be interpreted as an example of **cultural defence**. The group rejects 21st century **Global Culture** and wants to go back to the lifestyle and political arrangements of the 7th century CE: the time of the first Caliphate (Islamic empire) after the death of Muhammad. In this 'new Caliphate' many ideas from Global Culture (such as women's equality and tolerance of homosexuality and religious differences) were banned.

Most Muslims reacted with horror to ISIS's atrocities, but some in the Middle East who had experienced invasion by US/UK armies and the collapse of their traditional lifestyles were attracted to its promise to 'turn back the clock.' Because ISIS continued to use 21st century technology, like the Internet and weaponry, it could be seen as a **Hybrid Culture**, mixing ancient and modern ideas.

Because Islamic State tried to set up a country which launched attacks in Europe and Africa, this is also an example of **Political Globalisation**. They stole ancient treasures and oil which they sold on the worldwide black market so **Economic Globalisation** is at work too.

Research: Go back over your notes on **1A: Socialisation, Culture & Identity** and apply these ideas to **Global Culture**, **Consumer Culture**, **National Identities**, **Religion as an agency of social control**, the 'white wannabes' studied by **Nayak** and the debate over 'My Culture is Not Your Prom Dress.'

RESEARCH PROFILE: GIDDENS (1999) - continued

Anthony Giddens's book **Runaway World** *(1999) appears in* **1A: Socialisation, Culture & Identity** *and is expanded upon here. Because of its accessible style and the breadth of topics Giddens addresses, I'd say if an A-Level Sociology student intends to read* **just one book** *by a famous sociologist, it should be this one.*

Giddens identifies Globalisation as a force that changes the way we live, saying: *"We are the first generation to live in global society, whose contours we can as yet only dimly see. It is shaking up our existing ways of life, no matter where we happen to be."*

He discusses how Globalisation causes **de-traditionalisation** – where people question their traditional beliefs about religion, gender roles, etc. People often continue with traditional lifestyles, rather than actually changing them, but their cultures become unstable, because people are aware that there are alternative ways of living; they know that they can abandon their traditions if they want to whereas before Globalisation came along most people found abandoning traditions unthinkable.

When people **do** abandon their traditions, they develop a **'global outlook.'** Giddens calls this emerging global identity **'Cosmopolitanism'** (from the Greek *kosmos* meaning 'the world').

Giddens thinks this leads to **democratisation**: as tradition becomes less influential, people must work out for themselves the role that culture plays in their lives.

This leads to a lifestyle of constant questioning and re-evaluating, which Giddens calls **reflexivity**.

Giddens talks about **manufactured risks** – threats that result from our own runaway technology, like oil spills and nuclear reactor leaks, but also global warming. These risks haven't been around long enough for human beings to judge how big a threat they are or work out what to do about them. They are too big in scale for national governments to tackle singlehandedly. That's why Giddens says there is *"a new riskiness to risk."*

These factors combine to create cultural problems because the decline of tradition, new manufactured risks and constant need to re-evaluate overwhelms us.

Giddens thinks it leads some people to **addictions**, which are attempts to anchor yourself to something stable (the way tradition used to do). The other is **fundamentalism**, as people commit to a single blinkered set of beliefs and ignore (or try to destroy) all the confusing alternatives.

Giddens has a mixture of optimism and caution about Globalisation. However, he rejects the Postmodernist analysis. He claims we are still living in **Late Modernity**, not a new Postmodern society. We do not choose our own identities, instead we rely on **'expert systems'** – therapists, self-help books, online influences, celebrity role models, doctors and scientists. This falls somewhere between the structuralist view that we are controlled by social institutions and the Postmodernist view that we choose our own Identities.

Economic Globalisation

This is the way in which trade, banking and tourism have made different parts of the world depend on each other, creating some staggering inequalities as well as huge profits. This process goes back to the British Empire's creation of colonies in India and Africa and elsewhere. Often, resources (metals, woods, animals, fuels or just cheap labour) are taken from developing countries to make cheap goods in wealthy countries, while developing countries are sold other products (technology, medicines, entertainment, weaponry) that they would not otherwise produce themselves.

The mixture of examples above (medicines *and* weaponry) shows how difficult it is to agree on this aspect of Globalisation. Are developing countries being helped or exploited, protected or ruined?

Free Trade (Neoliberalism): This is the idea that, if everyone trades freely, everyone benefits. Many developing countries have resources they are not using that the rest of the world needs (minerals or oil underground, forests of valuable timber, fields for crops) and the developed countries have inventions that poor countries would benefit from (medicine, weapons to defend themselves). Why not swap? Critics point out that this trade is stacked in favour of the richer countries and the **Trans-National Corporations (TNCs)** and that poor countries often have their resources taken away (causing environmental damage) and get little back in return.

Protectionism: This is the idea that there should be barriers to free trade to protect local communities. It might mean charging **tariffs** (fees) on things being imported into a country, restricting immigration (especially migrant labour) or the government helping local industries (like factories or farms) so that they can compete with foreign industries that do things cheaper. In 2016, **Donald Trump** was elected US President with the slogan **'America First'** which referred to economic protectionism. This is like an economic version of 'cultural defence' which tries to resist the effects of Globalisation in a country.

Anti-globalisation protest (photo: John Englart)

11

AO2 ILLUSTRATION: THE ANTI-GLOBALISATION MOVEMENT

This is a protest movement that campaigns against Economic Globalisation. In 1999, protesters disrupted the meeting of the **World Trade Organisation (WTO)** in Seattle, USA. 600 were arrested and thousands injured in clashes with the police. The **World Social Forum** was created in 2001 to oppose the activities of groups like the WTO, the World Bank and meetings like the G8 where world leaders gathered to make global economic plans.

The anti-globalists are sometimes termed **'globalutionaries'** (global-revolutionaries) but term themselves the **Global Justice Movement**. They claim that **Neoliberalism** leads to the **destruction of the environment** (e.g. the cutting down of the Amazon Rainforest) and **war** (e.g. the US/UK invasion of Iraq in 2003). They argue these things happen because wealthy people (and TNCs) want the resources (especially oil) in poorer countries and are prepared to destroy the environment and trigger wars in order to get what they want.

However, some anti-globalists are **nationalists** who are concerned that their countries are being changed by immigration and their businesses are being closed down by foreign competition or else bought out by foreign companies. In recent years, many elections and referendums have shown that this protectionist feeling has grown stronger (e.g. the **2016 Brexit referendum**).

RESEARCH PROFILE: ROBINSON (2004)

William Robinson is a **Marxist** who argues a new capitalist class has emerged and a new transnational state exists outside of national borders. The new class are a 'global elite' of businesspeople (they are a *"transnational bourgeoisie"*) who have investments all over the world. They are not loyal to any particular country. Instead, they are part of a **transnational state**.

Robinson argues this transnational state and its global ruling class makes up the new 21st century Hegemony. These elites share the same lifestyles and are connected to each other socially. The gap between the rich and poor grows as the super-rich acquire more wealth. They are capable of manipulating or bullying national governments, so 'democracy' no longer means anything

Robinson argues that this Globalised Capitalism is really a world war: *"it is the war of a global rich and powerful minority against the global poor, dispossessed and outcast majority"* (1996).

This idea of a 'war' going on that no one acknowledges is classic **Conflict Theory**. However, Robinson's critics say his theory doesn't explain why wars between nation states continue or why nationalism is growing in popularity. His theory of a transnational bourgeoisie needs more evidence: the existence of super-rich people like **Jeff Bezos** or **Bill Gates** is obvious, but it's not clear they undermine democracy or exploit the poor in the way that Robinson says.

Robinson's view of Globalisation is similar to **Giddens'** view in some ways (e.g. greater **risk**, p9) but he rejects Giddens' idea that Globalisation is making the world more **democratic**; he thinks so-called democracy is an illusion and we are controlled by the transnational bourgeoisie.

Political Globalisation

For most of history, people have organised themselves into tribes, kingdoms or empires. Since the 18th century (the 'European Enlightenment'), these have been replaced with nation states. Nation states are made up of people with a common history and (usually) language and religion and defined by historic borders. Nation states have a central government that has a responsibility to defend its citizens and secure their wellbeing. **Functionalists** regard the nation state as the best political arrangement for human flourishing and view **National Identity** as important.

Globalisation has brought about **supra-national** ('above the nation') organisations. These are groups like the World Trade Organisation (WTO), the United Nations (UN), the European Union (EU) and the European Court of Human Rights (ECHR).

Supra-nationalism: This is the idea that nation states create many problems (e.g. they fight wars with each other) and are not well equipped to solve modern problems that go beyond their borders (e.g. international crime, global warming). The best solution is for nations to be supervised by larger bodies that impose international laws and make global decisions. Ultimately, such thinking goes, the nation states will fade away and be replaced by larger decision-making bodies – perhaps a single global government.

Nationalism: Nationalists support the nation state as the ideal political settlement, not despite its limitations but because of them: nation states provide freedom and democratic accountability through elections. Nationalists argue that a supra-national decision-making body would in fact be 'an empire' and empires have historically not been very concerned with the wellbeing of their populations. There is a recent surge in **ethno-nationalism**, which is the view that the best nation state is one that corresponds to a single **Ethnic Identity**: this has given support to independence movements in Scotland, Catalonia (Spain) and elsewhere, who argue that even broad national governments like the UK and Spain are not free or democratic enough.

AO2 ILLUSTRATION: THE GREAT FIREWALL OF CHINA

A firewall is a type of computer technology that stops people getting access to a website or database. It's usually to stop hackers getting access to private accounts. The Chinese Communist Party (CCP) has created the 'Great Firewall' stop prevent the population of China gaining access to many foreign websites and cut down on digital information going into or out of China. The point of this is to censor what Chinese people get to learn about. This makes the Great Firewall an example of **Cultural Defence** as well as the use of the Internet to control populations and silence free speech.

The Great Firewall was completed in 2008. It prevents Chinese Internet-users from accessing services like *Google* Search, *Facebook*, *Twitter*, *Wikipedia* (Chinese-language version) and *Amazon*. China has developed its own versions of these services, e.g. *Sina Weibo* (*Twitter*) and *QZone* (*Facebook*). This makes the Great Firewall a type of **Protectionism**.

AO2 ILLUSTRATION: THE EUROPEAN UNION

The **European Union (EU)** came into existence in 1993, formed out of the previous European Economic Community (EEC) of which the UK had been a member. The new EU was **a supra-national body** with its own parliament in which the member nations 'pooled their sovereignty' (i.e. gave up the power to make some decisions so the EU could make decisions for everyone).

The EU is a regulatory body, setting standards and laws for its members. Some of these rules benefit some countries more than others, but the idea was that members would gain more than they lost by pooling sovereignty. In 2012, the EU received the **Nobel Peace Prize** for advancing human rights.

Two EU regulations were particularly controversial. The **single currency (the Euro)** replaced many national currencies in 2002. A national currency (like the British Pound) is a symbol of **National Identity** and the UK did not adopt the Euro. **Free movement of labour** meant that EU workers could travel to any member country and seek work and claim benefits there. This was also seen by some people as a threat to National Identity, especially in the run-up to the **2016 EU (or 'Brexit') Referendum** in which the UK voted to 'Leave' the EU (52% compared to 48% 'Remain').

However, the EU was also supposed to function as a 'counterweight' to American and other global influences. For example, in 2016 the EU established **General Data Protection Regulation (GPDR)** which restricted what companies (including the trans-national 'Tech Giants') could do with private data.

This makes the EU a combination of **supra-nationalism** (since it takes powers from its member nations) and **nationalism** (since it resists the wider effects of Globalisation from outside Europe). The EU allows **free trade** between its member nations but charges tariffs on goods coming into the EU from outside, which is **protectionist** (p11). The culture the EU promotes can sometimes conflict with the culture of its member states, for example Poland's ban on abortion (2021) or Hungary's restricting of homosexuality (2021). By opposing these new laws, the EU is promoting **cultural homogeneity** (p6).

RESEARCH PROFILE: GOODHART (2017)

David Goodhart is a Functionalist who wrote *The Road To Somewhere* (2017) in which he argues that recent politics have been shaped by the presence of two large groups of people in society, which he terms the 'Anywheres' and the 'Somewheres' based on where they feel they live.

The **'Somewheres'** are people with a sense of belonging to a particular place: their home town or country. They tend to live in the countryside or small towns. They are typically less educated and distrust change; they are anxious about immigration and oppose the EU. They make up- about 50% of the UK population.

The **'Anywheres'** are people without this sense of belonging. They would be equally happy living 'anywhere' and don't feel particularly patriotic. They tend to be urban (city-based) and university educated; they are happy with immigration and pro-EU. They make up 20-25% of the population but include a lot of the 'elite' people (top politicians, broadcasters, businesspeople, celebrities) who travel widely and don't have a fixed home for long.

The rest of the population are **'Inbetweeners'** caught between the stay-put mentality of the 'Somewheres' and the footloose mentality of the 'Anywheres.'

Goodhart claims that the views of 'Somewheres' don't get expressed in the Media or in politics, so that (in his view) the **2016 EU Referendum** was a victory for the neglected 'Somewheres.'

Goodhart's views seem to link to the idea of **National Identity** and **cultural defence** (p8) and he presents these values as important to most of the UK population.

Goodhart's critics point out that a lot of UK newspapers support a 'Somewhere' mentality (being patriotic and anti-EU) so this isn't *really* a neglected group. Moreover, a lot of so-called 'Anywheres' *also* have a sense of home and community, but they are equally optimistic about immigration and international cooperation, so there isn't the sort of stark contrast between the two outlooks that Goodhart makes out.

Robinson would link the 'Anywheres' to the transnational bourgeoisie but would reject the idea that the EU Referendum was really a victory for the 'Somewheres' because he doesn't think independent nations like the UK are able to stand up to the transnational state.

Giddens (p9) would link the 'Anywheres' to the new **Cosmopolitan** outlook created by **detraditionalization** and that would suggest their numbers are bound to grow while the 'Somewheres' are going to shrink.

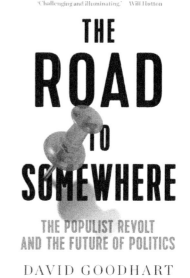

'Challenging and illuminating.' Will Hutton

THE ROAD TO SOMEWHERE

THE POPULIST REVOLT AND THE FUTURE OF POLITICS

DAVID GOODHART

Conclusions About Globalisation

Defining *"social relations"* as Cultural Globalisation explains a lot of important conflicts going on, such as the promoting of LGBT Pride in countries that had previously tended to be homophobic; it also explains the rise of religious fundamentalism, eating disorders and Internet conspiracy theories as people look for something to replace the sense of tradition that Globalisation has undermined.

However, not everyone experiences these cultural changes equally. Life in big cities is very multicultural, but lots of people live in the countryside or small towns, rather untouched by these changes. This links to **Goodhart**'s idea of the 'Anywheres' and the 'Somewheres' (p15).

Defining Globalisation as Economic explains *why* these changes are happening, especially if you accept **Robinson**'s view of the transnational bourgeoisie manipulating things behind the scenes (p12). People who experience the closure of a business in their community (when it lays off workers, relocates overseas and employs cheaper foreign workers) have a personal experience of this in action.

However, these economic changes don't predict everything and don't account for organisations like the **EU**, which is seen by some Marxists as a neoliberal organisation promoting free trade and Capitalism but viewed by others as an enemy of neoliberalism, promoting the regulation of big businesses and the welfare of workers (p14).

Defining Globalisation as Political links it to some of the big debates of recent years: Do governments have too much power or too little? Should we trust international courts more than our own? Should politicians listen when supra-national organisations like the UN criticise what they do? Was the UK right to leave the EU?

However, lots of people are quite apathetic about these political debates. **Robinson** would argue that national politics is really just a smokescreen to hide the *real* power of the transnational bourgeoisie: elections and referendums don't really change anything.

Other sociologists point out that Globalisation is happening at different speeds in different places: faster in cities than in the countryside, faster in wealthy countries than poor ones; it is resisted by some religious states (e.g. in the Muslim world) and the **Great Firewall of China** is a barrier to some aspects of Globalisation reaching the Chinese people (p13).

Postmodernists claim that Globalisation has transformed society into a new Postmodern form, in which **meta-narratives** have become redundant. This means no one theory can explain anything anymore and Globalisation will mean different things depending on who you are and how you experience it. However, **Giddens** responds that Postmodernity isn't happening; we are living in a **Late Modern** society (p9), and we can still make meaningful theories about things, including the definition of Globalisation.

EXAM PRACTICE: DEFINING GLOBALISATION

The OCR exam has three questions in **Paper 3 Section A**:

Source A	Source B
Globalisation allows developing countries to catch up with the wealthy industrialised nations through increased manufacturing, economic expansion, and improvements in standards of living. Big companies out-source jobs to developing countries which helps them to grow their economies. By removing barriers to trade, money flows across borders. Globalisation has advanced social justice by focusing attention on human rights worldwide, such as atrocities or the mistreatment of minorities or women, that might have otherwise been ignored.	For better and worse, globalisation has made the world less diverse. Starbucks, Nike and Gap dominate shopping centres all over the world. The sheer size and reach of America have made cultural exchange among nations largely a one-sided affair. Globalisation has created a concentration of wealth and power in the hands of a tiny elite that can gobble up smaller competitors around the globe. Poorer people suffer the disappearance of entire industries to new locations abroad and their politicians are powerless to prevent it.

1. With references to the Source[s], define what sociologists mean by globalisation.
   [9 marks: 5 AO1 + 4 AO2]

*Make two sociological points about globalisation, one based on Source A and one on Source B. You should quote from the source. It's not vital to refer to named sociologists but you should definitely use some sociological terminology. Then offer examples of globalisation and makes sure each example has an explanation of **why** it is globalisation. For example, "Buying junk food because it's sold by transnational corporations that advertise on TV."*

2. With references to the Source[s], to what extent have sociologists successfully defined globalisation? **[10 marks: 4 AO1 + 2 AO2 + 4 AO3]**

Write a paragraph about source A then another about source B. Sum up what's in the source and explain what named sociologists would say about it. Then finish off with a brief evaluation (p65) of each view. Make sure you conclude by answering the question (they have defined it or they haven't or they've partially defined it).

3. Evaluate the view that globalisation cannot be satisfactorily defined. **[16 marks: 4 AO1 + 4 AO2 + 8 AO3]**

*Write three paragraphs. Each paragraph should introduce a sociological idea with some illustration from the real world. Each paragraph should finish off with developed evaluation (see **Chapter 4** for this). For example, you could write about the defining globalisation in cultural terms; then the economic definition, then finish off with the political definition. Don't forget to answer the question: is it possible to define this process of globalisation satisfactorily?*

17

CHAPTER TWO – DIGITAL COMMUNICATION

This part of the course has the full title **'the relationship between globalisation and digital forms of communication.'**

*The phrase **'digital forms of communication'** is going to be used A LOT and, now that I've introduced it, I shall use the abbreviation **DFOC**. I recommend you do too. Just remember to use the full phrase at the start of an essay to introduce the abbreviation to the Examiner.*

Digital information is information stored in the form of numbers – in effect, computer code. A machine then translates this digital information into something you can make sense of, like an image on a screen or sound from speakers. That's how your mobile phone works.

Older technology uses **analogue** rather than digital information. Analogue means 'representation' (as in the word 'analogy'). Think of a watch where the second hand sweeps round the dial: it is *representing* the passage of time.

Analog is also a word used generally to represent **non-digital communication**. This includes writing things in physical books or letters, printed newspapers and magazines and of course vinyl records.

Vinyl record (photo: Anders Printz)

Think of the advantages of digital music (e.g. mp3 files, songs streamed from Spotify or downloaded from iTunes Store): it doesn't take up any physical space, it cannot be broken or stolen, it's easy to find, it doesn't crackle or hiss, you can manipulate it (such as cutting it up or adding it to a video soundtrack).

Now think of the disadvantages: you can't touch it or look at it, you don't feel as though you own it in the way you own a vinyl record on your shelf, many people feel the sound quality is inferior (it sounds less 'real' than an analogue recording).

The switch to **DFOC (digital forms of communication)** is an important part of Globalisation, because digital information can be sent around the world so much faster and more reliably than analogue recordings.

Positive Views of Digital Forms of Communication

DFOC involves nearly instantaneous transferral of information. The information is broken down into numbers, transferred electronically and reconstructed at the other end. Satellite link-ups mean that the information can be sent all around the world and WiFi means you don't need to be physically connected by a wire or cable to have access to digital information.

Digital information can be copied multiple times with no loss of quality. This means that far more people can all communicate at once, instantaneously, compared to what used to be possible with analogue technology (think of the audience voting on shows like *Strictly Come Dancing*). Digital information can be manipulated (think of what *TikTok* lets you do with a video or how *Photoshop* can alter an image). This ability to manipulate digital information means DFOC is much more interactive than the old analogue sort: if you read a book, the most you can do to interact with it is to write in the margins but if you read a website you can click on hyperlinks taking you to other sites, videos or pop-up captions.

DFOC represents a huge leap forward in human communication, massively increasing the number of people we can communicate with and our ability to interact with them. This ought to be very **empowering** technology for ordinary people.

Negative Views of Digital Forms of Communication

DFOC comes with its own risks, mostly linked to lack of authenticity. The ability to copy digital information creates problems of piracy and fakes. It's much more difficult to assert ownership of digital products, which can be copied and shared millions of times. Digital property can be hacked and digital identities can be stolen. This has led to the problem of unrealistic photoshopped images, 'Fake News' and 'Deep Fake' videos making it hard to tell what's real and what's not.

Critics are concerned that the interactivity involved in DFOC can lead to destructive behaviour. For example, some people maliciously create computer viruses and spread them through DFOC. This is a threat to the privacy and security of ordinary people, but cyber-hacking also threatens national security and is a new type of terrorism and warfare.

Ordinary people behave differently when communicating digitally, leading to problems like online 'Trolls' who threaten and insult strangers or 'Revenge Porn' where jilted lovers upload sexual images of their exes. DFOC makes it very difficult to shield children from violent or pornographic material and means they are not safe from bullying even in their own home.

DFOC adds to the risk of life in the 21st century society, creating more opportunities for crime, antisocial behaviour and confusion. It adds to the stress of modern life, especially for young people, and creates a crisis over what information can be trusted.

Research: Go back over your notes on **1A: Socialisation, Culture & Identity** and apply these ideas to the 77th Brigade of military cyber-warfare; find out about Deep Fakes and Fake News, problems with trolls and the spread of Internet hoaxes and conspiracy theories

Relationship to Social Capital

Social capital refers to the networks of people that enable society to function. 'Capital' normally means 'wealth' so having social capital means having connections that empower you: friends in high places, people with skills that can help you out, favours you can call in, a support group, people who value you and back you up. It includes fame and popularity but also skills like etiquette that enable you to get the best interactions from strangers, such as being able to persuade the police not to arrest you or talk an employer into giving you a job.

> **Research:** Go back over your notes on **1A: Socialisation, Culture & Identity** and apply these ideas to **Bourdieu**'s theory of **cultural capital** and the **Great British Class Survey** which incorporated the idea of social capital into its classifications

DFOC has changed the nature of social capital. You could be very socially isolated person but have lots of online friends and followers. You could have online links to influential or famous people whom you could never meet in real life. Online social capital can help you get jobs, find romance or exert political power, such as campaigning against a celebrity or a company to demand an apology or a change of policy.

Some people can 'monetise' their DFOC, getting earnings through adverts on their channel or endorsing products or brands. This has led to the rise of online influencers.

Zoella (photo: Gage Skidmore)

AO2 ILLUSTRATION: ZOELLA

Zoe Sugg (b. 1990) started a fashion blog when she was 19 that turned into the **Zoella** YouTube channel in 2009, amassing over 10 million subscribers. She films fashion ideas, shopping 'hauls' and vlogs (video blogging) about her daily life as 'Zoella.' In 2013 she was recognised as one of Britain's most influential Tweeters for her Twitter feed and in 2013 she helped launch the **National Citizens Service (NCS)** and became a digital ambassador for the mental health charity Mind. She has since branched out into beauty products, writing books and TV appearances.

Along with her brother (and fellow YouTuber) **Joe Sugg**, Zoe Sugg was nominated as Social Media Superstar at the 2019 Global Awards.

Zoe Sugg is a good example of a young person acquiring huge social capital through DFOC and then monetising that influence into economic capital (she was estimated to be worth over £4 million in 2021).

Research: Go back over your notes on **1A: Socialisation, Culture & Identity** and apply these ideas to **Global Culture** and agencies of **secondary socialisation**; research other online influencers and some of the controversies surrounding them

Not everyone agrees that DFOC increases social capital. You need to be familiar with the Internet's technology, which excludes many older people as well as people who cannot afford the equipment and software needed to promote themselves online or make the time to do it (perhaps, because they have family or working commitments). Online social capital is easily lost once your followers desert you and online celebrities are vulnerable to threats by '**Trolls**' (p59) as well as stalking.

Other critics point out the online social capital comes at the expense of the offline sort: more time spent blogging, tweeting and cultivating your online presence means less time socialising with friends, volunteering for local causes or attending evening classes or live entertainment with other people. **Functionalists** in particular think there is a quality to real-life interactions that is missing online and they worry that online social capital does not bring about social solidarity in the way that engaging with real people does.

RESEARCH PROFILE: PUTNAM (2000)

Robert Putnam wrote *Bowling Alone* (2000) in which he argues that social capital in the USA has been declining since the 1960s. He carries out a lot of statistical analysis on various measures of social engagement: voting, giving blood, going to church, joining community organisations (e.g. local charities, school boards) and sporting leagues – all are going down every year.

The title of the book comes from the fact that, though more people are going bowling, fewer people take part in organised bowling leagues: they are 'bowling alone.'

Putnam blames this change on several factors, like people moving to the suburbs far away from social venues, the rise in watching TV as a pastime and the generation gap (with young people less inclined to join organisations than their parents and grandparents).

Of course, Putnam can be criticised for only describing the USA. Things might be different in Europe and the UK. However, the biggest criticism is that Putnam ignores the appearance of the Internet. Are people replacing social capital in the offline world with online social capital instead?

Geraci et al. (2018) studies UK Internet-users with fast-speed broadband and concludes that having fast-speed Internet access links to declining participation in social activities, just as Putnam argued was happening in the USA. However, this ignores the possibility that users are replacing their offline social capital with different (and perhaps better) online social capital.

PERSPECTIVES ON DIGITAL COMMUNICATION

Functionalists, who believe in an important biological component to people's social experiences and society's needs, tend to be sceptical of DFOC as a substitute for face-to-face interactions. Other sociological Perspectives look at this new way of interacting differently.

POSTMODERN PERSPECTIVE: POSTMODERNISM

The **Postmodernist** Perspective was introduced in **Paper 1 Section B**. It is a complex set of loosely related ideas originating from the radical ideas of a group of (mainly French) thinkers in the 1960s and '70s. It proposes that the MODERNITY that emerged in the 18th century (the European Enlightenment) is collapsing and being replaced by a new POSTMODERNITY. This Postmodernity is characterised by intense **individualism** and **choice**, the **fragmentation** of old social structures, **diversity** in society and **fluidity** in identities.

Postmodernists see Globalisation as an important driver of Postmodernity: the new **Global Culture** forces everyone to pick and choose how they want to construct their identity and calls traditional lifestyles into question by exposing us to the alternatives out there.

The other driver of Postmodernity is **Media Saturation**: we are bombarded by media images from TV, films, the Internet, etc. and this media overdose changes the way we view reality itself. **Baudrillard (1970)** claims we live now in a confusing **Hyper Reality** where media images are more important than real experiences; **Lyotard (1979)** argues that this state of affairs makes it impossible to believe anything you are presented with is the absolute truth.

Research: Go back over your notes on **1A: Socialisation, Culture & Identity** and remind yourself about **Baudrillard** and then refresh your understanding of Postmodernism from your notes on **Paper 1 Section B**, including **Giddens**' argument that, instead of Postmodernity, we are living in risk-filled Late Modernity.

DFOC appeared in the 1990s and 2000s, long after most Postmodern theories, but they have created *exactly* the sort of conditions that Postmodernists warned were coming.

- DFOC encourages **individualism**, by letting people create their own online identities with groups of friends very different from their offline life
- DFOC encourages **choice** by offering a huge range of products, fashions, ideas and lifestyles – and because DFOC are more interactive, individuals can exercise choices online that they couldn't offline.
- DFOC leads to **fragmentation** as people increasingly live in a social media 'bubble' in contact with like-minded people and lose contact with people who don't share their views
- DFOC leads to more **diverse and fluid identities**, because you can reinvent yourself online as someone new

CONFLICT PERSPECTIVE: MARXISM

Marxism is a Conflict Perspective because it views society as a conflict between the powerless working classes and the ruling class who own all the resources. **Neo-Marxism** has developed this simple idea by suggesting that instead of an identifiable group of rulers (the '**bourgeoisie**') there is a collection of privileged interests in society called **Hegemony**. We have already studied **Robinson**'s idea (p12) that Globalisation has created a new global elite, the **transnational bourgeoisie**, that is waging an economic war against the rest of the human population.

Traditionally, Marxism has been a MATERIALIST philosophy that was concerned about physical wealth (in the form of land, factories and resources like steel and coal) and who controlled these things. From this materialist perspective, DFOC seems rather unimportant: it's just like ordinary communication, only faster and more far-reaching, but the important stuff of people being exploited and the mission to resist Capitalism is going on in the real world.

Intersectionality & Neo-Marxism

Intersectionality is the idea that a person possesses privileged or oppressed identities which can intersect. For example, your White Ethnic Identity confers privileges ("**white privilege**") but your Working Class Identity and your LGBT Sexual Identity intersect with this and cause you to experience victimhood in a more intense way.

Neo-Marxists are in the Marxist tradition of seeing society as in conflict because of Capitalism, but they abandon Marx's strict division of the working and ruling classes in favour of Antonio Gramsci's idea of **hegemonic groups** – groups that want to keep their privileges by keeping other groups down. This enables Neo-Marxists to move beyond issues of class to be concerned about other forms of oppression and marginalisation (e.g. racism, homophobia, transphobia, etc.).

For example, Neo-Marxists have been alerted to how Western societies (i.e. the UK, Europe, America) have a **postcolonial** outlook– they view themselves as superior because they once ruled over other cultures and this sense of superiority is expressed in everyday attitudes. Concerns over **cultural appropriation** and the philosophy behind **#BlackLivesMatter** (see p26) come from this Perspective (as well as others). Neo-Marxists argue that Western society needs to be **de-colonised** by removing the privileges enjoyed by White people and incorporating the voices and perspectives of non-White communities.

This has led to the development of **Social Justice** in politics (p52). Critics complain that it has taken the focus away from the original concern of Marxism: the working class and their struggle against the ruling class.

A shift from materialist Marxism to a more linguistic focus influenced by Postmodernism has led to ***Post-Marxism*** *(p41) – this is discussed in* ***Chapter 3****.*

Research: Go back over your notes on **1A: Socialisation, Culture & Identity** refresh your understanding of **Intersectionality**.

CONFLICT PERSPECTIVE: FEMINISM

Feminism is a Conflict Perspective which discerns in society the oppression and subordination (i.e. making them less important) of women by men. The male domination of society is termed Patriarchy and as well as the literal wealth, strength and political power men enjoy this also includes an **ideology** that represents male dominance as 'natural' and which hides and justifies the mistreatment of women.

Feminism has been through at least four 'waves':

- **1st Wave Feminism** in the 19th and early 20th century includes the Suffragettes who campaigned for women to have the right to vote, be educated and inherit property.
- **2nd Wave Feminism** in the 1960s and '70s campaigned for equality in other areas and reforms to society such as the freedom to divorce, access to contraception and abortion and changing attitudes towards sexual harassment and domestic violence. It includes liberal feminists (who want equality with men) and radical feminists (who want to change the way women live in society in a more fundamental way).

These Feminists were MATERIALISTS in a similar way to traditional Marxists: they focused on factors like economic inequality, violence to women, childcare, reproductive rights and women's bodies. From this materialist perspective, DFOC does not seem important: even if women can conduct themselves with freedom online, it doesn't change the material realities of life for women in the real world.

I try to avoid contrasting DFOC with 'the real world' since online experiences are 'real' too. However, I do use 'the real world' when discussing materialist perspectives, because they do regard DFOC as less 'real' than offline material circumstances.

Intersectionality & later Waves of Feminism

Intersectionality originates with **Kimberley Crenshaw**'s *Mapping The Margins* (**1991**) and was quickly adapted by many Feminists. This focus on oppressed or marginalised Identities influenced two more 'waves' of Feminism:

- **3rd Wave Feminism** in the 1990s and 2000s developed an intersectional view of privilege and oppression, with womanhood being one marginalised Identity among others, but intersecting Identities (such as Black women or LGBT women) experiencing oppression that is particularly intense and distinctive.
- **4th Wave Feminism** is often considered to start in 2012 with the launch of Laura Bates' **Everyday Sexism Project** (**https://everydaysexism.com**) which encouraged women to share their testimonies of sexual harassment and assault. This perspective is linked to Gender Identity Theory.

Intersectionality criticises earlier forms of Feminism as being too concerned with the experiences of White women (perhaps, middle class, able-bodied, straight, White women in particular). This new perspective revitalised Feminism in the 1990s and gave 3rd Wave Feminism a new focus.

3rd Wave Feminism also merges with Neo-Marxism in the **Social Justice** movement, encouraging a shared concern for all sorts of oppressed groups, not just the struggle of women.

As with Neo-Marxism, this leads to the criticism that 3rd Wave Feminism is taking its focus away from the original concern of Feminism: women and what unites them, their common experience of subordination to men in a Patriarchal society.

For example, one feature of 3rd Wave Feminism has been a re-think about **prostitution** and **pornography**. Earlier materialist Feminists saw these as social evils and examples of women being exploited by men. Some 3rd Wave Feminists argue that taking part in prostitution or pornography is **empowering** for some women and they argue that it is a judgmental attitude towards sex and the female body that *really* oppresses women. This view is called **sex-positivity** and the sex-positive movement calls for making sex safer, healthier and consensual rather than trying to ban sexual activities. This 3rd Wave view that prostitution should be legalised is opposed by materialist Feminists like **Julie Bindel (2017)** who argue that *"prostitution is inherently abusive, and a cause and a consequence of women's inequality."*

4th Wave Feminism can be hard to distinguish from 3rd Wave Feminism, but the main feature is its focus on the Internet for activism. It has been called *"3rd Wave Feminism with apps"* (**Rod Liddle, 2021**) or *"hashtag Feminism"* (**Jessica Bennett, 2014**, *c.f.* p26).

One of the targets of 4th Wave Feminism is **rape culture** – the idea that ordinary culture is dominated by norms and values that justify male violence and sexual assault on women and this is seen in media images and practices like victim-blaming and 'slut-shaming.'

A shift from materialist Feminism to a more linguistic focus influenced by Postmodernism has led to **Gender Identity Theory** *(p53) – this is discussed in* **Chapter 3**.

Hashtags (photo: nina_pic)

Research: Go back over your notes on **1A: Socialisation, Culture & Identity** and update your understanding of **3rd** and **4th Wave Feminism**

AO2 ILLUSTRATION: HASHTAGS

A hashtag is a word or phrase on social media preceded by the hash symbol (#) that makes a message easy to find. Their use started on Twitter in 2007 but the word hashtag entered the Oxford English Dictionary in 2014.

#EverydaySexism was used by **Laura Bates** in 2012 to encourage women to share their testimonies of being ignored, insulted, harassed or assaulted by men. Within 3 years, 100,000 testimonies had been posted from women all over the world.

In 2013, the hashtag **#KillAllMen** caused controversy when it trended. However, the users were not calling for violence; they were mostly women complaining on social media of being catcalled or sex pestered by men.

In 2017, news broke of multiple accusations of sexual assault against the film maker Harvey Weinstein. The actor **Alyssa Milano** wrote: *"If all the women who have been sexually harassed or assaulted wrote 'Me too' as a status, we might give people a sense of the magnitude of the problem."* Soon, accounts of sexual abuse from women with the hashtag **#MeToo** numbered in the millions.

The hashtag **#BlackLivesMatter** first appeared in 2013, following the acquittal of a US policeman for shooting a Black suspect, **Trayvon Martin**. In the next 5 years it was used 30 million times on Twitter. It trended again in 2020 after the murder of **George Floyd** by a US police officer. The hashtag became a slogan for anti-racism protesters in over 60 countries.

This shows the power of DFOC to draw attention to a cause and how it can spread into offline protests and political action.

#MeToo & #WeTogether (photo: Jeanne Menjoulet)

DIGITAL COMMUNICATION: A TOOLKIT

Digital Forms of Communication (DFOC) include text messages, emails, social media posts, blogs, podcasts, *YouTube* and *TikTok* videos and interactive websites.

Because of the choice and interactivity DFOC offers, this is evidence for the predictions of **Postmodernists** about living in a new age characterised by **media saturation**, **choice** and **fluid identities**. Traditional (**materialist**) **Marxists** and **Feminists** are sceptical about this, pointing out that important inequalities continue to exist in the 'real' world. However, **Neo-Marxists** and **4th Wave Feminists**, who share an **Intersectionality** outlook, think that language itself (**hegemonic discourse**) is the main force that sustains inequality – and these discourses can be revealed and challenged online.

THE DIGITAL REVOLUTION

The **Digital Revolution** has been termed the **Third Industrial Revolution** (after the Agricultural Revolution changed farming and the Industrial Revolution changed manufacturing). It can be dated from **1989**, the year **Tim Berners-Lee** invented the **World Wide Web**.

By the early 2000s, mobile phones and text messaging became commonplace. As of 2020, 67% of the world's population is connected to the Internet. Shopping, banking and even dating have increasingly moved online and, during the **2020 Coronavirus Pandemic**, working and studying from home involved access to the Internet using webcams and live video streaming.

The new DFOC has led to the emergence of New Media, including (1) the **extension of traditional media** like film, TV, newspapers and books through digital formats such as streaming services (e.g. Netflix, BBC iPlayer), apps and e-readers; (2) **new platforms** for media, such as smartphones, tablets and laptops that let people take advantage of the interactive features of DFOC (such as uploading their own videos or maintaining their own social media feed).

AO2 ILLUSTRATION: THE WORLD WIDE WEB

The Internet is a vast number of computers connected together, but the **World Wide Web** is all the web pages that can be found on the Internet. It was invented in 1989 when British scientist **Tim Berners-Lee** developed the systems to enable computers to communicate, in particular URL addresses and HTML coding for creating web pages and HTTP for linking them. Berners-Lee did this to help scientists share research documents, but the Web opened up to the public in 1991.

At first, web pages were quite simple documents with pictures and text – not much different from the pages of magazines but with hyperlinks connecting them. From 2004, **Web 2.0** developed. This new version of the Web is much more interactive and allows users to post up their own content without needing to know computer programming languages. This has led to the rise of social media and the big 'Tech Giants' like **Google**, **Facebook** and **Twitter**.

RESEARCH PROFILE: CORNFORD & ROBINS (1999)

Is the Digital Revolution really a 'revolution'? **Cornford & Robins (1999)** argue that the New Media are **evolutionary**, rather than **revolutionary**. In other words, they are a progression from what already existed, but not a brand-new experience. Interactivity was present in traditional media, such as the letters pages in newspapers, or phoning in to radio or TV programmes. They argue that DFOC have made this interaction faster and easier but that is all.

Cornford & Robins also argue that DFOC will not revolutionise society either. The same sort of Capitalists control the New Media as controlled the old media. They are only concerned with making a profit and they use the New Media to spread **ruling class ideology** and **manufacture consent** to the Capitalist system. The 'choice' and 'interactivity' offered through DFOC is largely an illusion or confined to trivial matters, not important matters of wealth and power.

Cornford & Robins are coming from a traditional (**materialist**) **Marxist** Perspective (p23) – hence their scepticism about the Digital Revolution. Notice the publication date (1999) is from *before* Web2.0 and you could argue this makes their criticisms out-of-date because they only apply to the less-interactive world of the first **World Wide Web** (p27).

Research: technologies that contributed to the Digital Revolution (dial-up modems, broadband, smartphones, 5G, etc.)

THE GLOBAL VILLAGE

The **Global Village** is a phrase that puts across the link between Globalisation and the Digital Revolution: DFOC has 'shrunk the world' to make it like living in a village. In village life, everyone can know who everyone else is; they can communicate easily, share problems, work together on projects. They also share the same disasters and are equally affected by antisocial behaviour. No one is anonymous or uninvolved.

DFOC has created this Global Village by putting people in touch with (potentially) every other person on the planet. As with village life, we are able to share problems and get help (such as working together on climate control or applying for jobs in other countries).

We are also exposed to each other's problems, such as the rise on international terrorism and crime made possible by DFOC. This links to the idea of **manufactured risk (Giddens**, p9).

The concept of a Global Village also links to Giddens' ideas of **de-traditionalisation** and **cosmopolitanism** (p9) and the conflict detected by Goodhart between **'Somewheres' and 'Anywheres'** (p15).

AO2 ILLUSTRATION: ZHU LING'S MYSTERY ILLNESS

In 1995, **Zhu Ling**, a young science student at Beijing University, fell mysteriously ill. Doctors were unable to treat her and, as her condition worsened, her friends appealed for help on the Web (this was before the **Great Firewall** existed, p13). Over 1500 responses flooded in from around the world and a third correctly diagnosed thallotoxicosis, a rare condition caused by exposure to the element **Thallium**. Zhu Ling was treated using advice from doctors in many countries and made a partial recovery. The mystery of how and why Zhu Ling was poisoned with Thallium is still unsolved but this was a milestone case in 'remote diagnosis' by DFOC and an example of the Global Village at its best.

RESEARCH PROFILE: McLUHAN (1964)

The term 'Global Village' was coined by the Canadian commentator **Marshall McLuhan** in the 1960s, a long time before the **Digital Revolution** itself. McLuhan was farsighted in seeing where **Globalisation** was heading even without DFOC. McLuhan argues that due to communication technology *"the whole civilized world is made the psychological equivalent of a primitive tribe."* He suggests that this will bring about the **end of individualism** – whereas Postmodernists usually claim DFOC intensify individualism.

McLuhan ponders the good and bad sides of this. He argues that the Global Village is *"fission, not fusion"* – in other words, we will experience all this conflicts, rivalries and feuds of village life but on a global scale, rather than happy and harmonious integration.

McLuhan also famously stated *"**the medium is the message**."* This means that the qualities of a medium have as much effect as the information it communicates. For example, reading a description of an event in a newspaper has a different effect from hearing about it, or seeing a picture of it, or watching a video.

The idea that 'the medium is the message' is useful to criticise **Cornford & Robins** *(p28) because it suggests the interactive DFOC of Web2.0 will affect people differently from the old-fashioned electronic communications they were discussing. It will also be useful when we look at the* **Impact of Digital Communication** *(p38).*

NETWORKED GLOBAL SOCIETY

Social networks are another term for **social capital** (p20): they are the links you have to other people who can provide you with information, resources, financial or emotional support. Social networks include your friendship groups, your work colleagues, your family and people you know through hobbies, pastimes, clubs, political organisations or religion. **'Networking'** has become a word for increasing the usefulness of your social network.

As well as personal networks, there are now Digital Social Networks of contacts online. This has created a **Networked Global Society** on a worldwide scale, thanks to the **World Wide Web** (p27) and DFOC. These networks can be more powerful than the local networks of people you know personally and meet face-to-face. For example, if you are looking for a job you might ask family, friends and neighbours – your local network. But if you have a global network, people might tell you about job opportunities in other countries.

Most networks are **horizontal**, putting you in touch with people connected to you for different reasons (e.g. ex-girlfriends, former co-workers, old schoolfriends, people who share your memes). **Vertical networks** are people linked by a particular interest, like taste in music, career, age or hobby. Vertical networks include **ResearchGate** (a network for academics and researchers) or **Mumsnet** (for women and parents, p53). Since 2020, vertical network sites having been gaining members and horizontal network sites have been losing them. The advantage of vertical networks is that they filter out material that is irrelevant to you (holiday photos, pictures of cats, out-of-date memes) or opinions you don't like.

*Vertical networks will be important later on when you study **Impacts of Digital Communication** (p38) and debates around social media bubbles and echo chambers.*

AO2 ILLUSTRATION: LINKEDIN

LinkedIn is a networking site launched in 2002. It is rather more vertical than sites like *Facebook* or *Twitter*, because it's a professional network site to help people find jobs or recruit new employees. The focus is on sharing your work-related achievements and your LinkedIn profile functions as a CV, advertising your career history, qualifications and testimonials.

As of 2021, *LinkedIn* has over 750 million members from 200 countries. However, because it is an all-purpose professional network site, it is less vertical than *Goodwall*, which is specifically for people at the start of their careers looking for opportunities.

Research: other networking sites and how they are used: try Behance and StackOverflow as well as ResearchGate, Goodwall, Goodreads, BlogHer, Dribbble, Letterboxd, Mumsnet and others.

RESEARCH PROFILE: CASTELLS (2000)

Manuel Castells is a (former) Marxist sociologist who wrote *The Information Age* (a trilogy of books, concluding in **2000**). Castells argues that a new kind of Capitalism that he calls '**Global Informational Capitalism**' (or *'Informationalism'*) has emerged. This new Capitalism has shifted away from directly controlling oil, gas, coal or the factories that use them in favour of controlling information through global networks.

These networks are global in scale and very fluid: they bring together experts to complete a project then disperse them, rather than maintaining a workforce with a wage. Ordinary people, with little mobility, education or special skills, are excluded from these networks.

Castells argues we now live in an **Information Age** which can *"unleash the power of the mind"* and lead to more productivity, more leisure and less waste of resources if it can be managed properly (which involves challenging Global Informational Capitalism, which only cares about its own power and profits).

This network of elite Capitalists resembles the **transnational bourgeoisie** described by **Robinson** (p12). It is similar to the argument by **Cornford & Robins** (p28) that the arrival of DFOC has not changed the essential nature of Capitalism, because the Capitalist ruling class has adapted to it and uses it to maintain their own privilege and exclude everyone else. Castell's idea of the new Information Age has similarities to **Postmodernism**'s claim that society has entered a new phase.

MEDIA CONVERGENCE

Media convergence is the way different kinds of media that originally had their own distinctive platforms now come combined on a single platform.

For example, people used to get their radio broadcasts through a radio, their TV through a television set, their print news through a newspaper and their novels through books, while going to a cinema to see the latest films and listening to music on vinyl records.

Nowadays, all of these media can be accessed through apps on a tablet or smartphone: TV and radio can be streamed through apps like BBC iPlayer, most newspapers have subscription apps and there are new online news services, books can be read (or listened to) through e-reader apps like Kindle and music can be streamed through services like Spotify.

This means that when people access one type of media, they tend to get the whole converged package that goes with it. This creates **cultural convergence**; the emergence of a **Global Culture** based around Western (European and North American) TV, film, music and sport. This supports the Capitalist system that creates this technology, because you need to own these expensive smartphones and computers to access the media products.

AO2 ILLUSTRATION: AMAZON

Amazon started out as an online shopping website, founded by **Jeff Bezos** out of his garage in Seattle, USA. It began as an online bookstore in 1995. The website soon moved to sell more than just books and in 2007 *Amazon* release the ***Kindle*** e-reader. By 2010, customers were buying more e-books than physical books from *Amazon*.

In 2011, ***Amazon Video*** started selling and renting digital film and TV shows. In 2014, the ***Echo*** became the latest example of media convergence, being a device that can respond to voice commands (through its AI named '*Alexa*') to access music, audiobooks, podcasts and websites as well as operate other linked technology, such as the ***Amazon Prime*** TV channels. Since 2015, *Amazon* has produced its own films and TV series.

Amazon is a powerful example of **media convergence**, but has been criticised for driving out smaller competitors, destroying High Street shopping and treating its van drivers and warehouse workers poorly. Its success has made Jeff Bezos the richest person in the world (worth $200 billion in 2021).

Research: go back over your notes from **1A: Socialisation, Culture & Identity** and link these ideas to the Amazon workplace and secondary socialisation

RESEARCH PROFILE: BOYLE (2007)

Raymond Boyle (**2007**) argues that media like television has changed from being **supply-led** to being **demand-led** because of the **interactivity** in DFOC. For example, we are no longer limited by TV schedules. We can 'binge watch' entire series and options like 'the red button' let viewers construct their own viewing experience. Because of streaming services, viewers can watch shows at times that suit them and catch-up services let them access shows they would otherwise have missed.

All these media services can now be accessed through a single device, like a Smart TV, tablet or smartphone. Media is more interactive, allowing viewers to schedule their own entertainment with 'watchlists' and 'favourites' and media providers offer suggestions based on previous viewing.

This focus on the **choice** provided by media convergence links with a **Postmodernist** view. However, the tendency of media providers to offer more of what you've already seen can end up limiting your choice, which is an example of the risk pointed out by **Giddens** (p9).

*Notice the dates of Boyle's research: he's talking about the effect of **Web2.0** (p27) and doesn't suffer from being out-of-date like **Cornford & Robins** (p28).*

SOCIAL MEDIA

Digital Social Networks in the early years of the **World Wide Web** (p27) allowed users to post up comments and replies on bulletin boards on web pages. Since the arrival of **Web2.0**, users can upload their own multimedia content (images, videos, etc.) creating **Social Media**. This includes fully interactive services like Facebook, Instagram and Twitter.

Individuals use Social Media to stay in touch with family and friends and their wider community. Businesses use social media to market their products to customers. There is a lot of overlap between the two, especially as the interactivity of DFOC allows customers to leave comments and feedback on products or individuals to promote themselves like a business (for example, selling their helpful A-Level Study Guides).

Because of the **Networked Global Society** (p29), the reach of Social Media goes far beyond your home town or country. This means families can stay in touch around the world and businesses can market their products in other countries. It also means terrorists and criminals can plan their crimes on a much wider scale.

Because of **Media Convergence** (p31), Social Media tends to overlap with offline life: people upload phots of their meals or interrupt conversations to check updates. This blurring of the distinction between the online and offline links to **Postmodernist** ideas about **media saturation** and **Hyper Reality** (p22).

AO2 ILLUSTRATION: TWITTER AND TWITTER-STORMS

Twitter is a Social Media service that was launched in 2006. Users can post short (140 character) messages and links which form long threads of conversation, often identified by **hashtags** (p26). In 2020, there were 186 million *Twitter* users, with the most popular accounts (in terms of followers) being former US President Barack Obama and pop stars Katy Perry and Justin Bieber.

*The fact that 38 million Twitter users are American and the top accounts are all American celebrities reveals the US-bias in **Global Networked Society**.*

Twitter is used by many politicians, journalists and businesses to reach the public in a more direct way than ordinary press statements or adverts. It is also used by activists and protestors trying to draw attention to their causes. A **Twitter-storm** is a spike in posts around a particular topic or hashtag, usually taking the form of complaints and arguments. These 'storms' often make it into national news and cause politicians to change policies, public figures to issue apologies or businesses to drop clients. A **'pile-on'** is when lots of Internet-users get involved in such a storm, heaping criticism on one particular user for their views.

Twitter is called upon to **regulate** Tweets that are hateful or deceitful (p39). In 2021, US President **Donald Trump** was banned from *Twitter*, for inciting violence and making false allegations of voter fraud. However, abusive behaviour continues unchecked on *Twitter* – *c.f.* **Trolls & Incels** (p59).

RESEARCH PROFILE: RONSON (2015)

Jon Ronson's book *So You've Been Publicly Shamed* (**2015**) studies Twitter-storms and public shaming. Ronson reflects on his own experience of shaming a 'spambot' account that was copying his Tweets and interviews others who were at the centre of Twitter-storms, either as instigators (e.g. a woman who showed co-workers making sexist jokes and this led to one of them being sacked and then the woman losing her job too) or victims of these online outrages. The target of the public shaming is at the centre of an online 'pile-on' which can include abuse and threats, even death threats and (for women) rape threats.

Ronson argues that public shaming has a long history, especially in the USA. It was phased out as a punishment as ruining a person's reputation was increasingly seen as cruel. However, Ronson argues that DFOC has led to *"a great renaissance in public shaming."* The idea that online behaviour serves a social function – and one that is very old but in a new form – is a **Functionalist** insight. **Feminists** and **Marxists** argue that public shaming is an effective way for ordinary or marginalised people to call very powerful and privileged people to account in a way that would not be possible otherwise. **Postmodernists** view the volatile nature of DFOC as part of the fragmented nature of postmodernity.

Bor & Peterson (2021) explain this behaviour with the Functionalist **Mismatch Hypothesis**: mismatches between DFOC and human psychology mean that relationships become dysfunctional without face-to-face meetings

VIRTUAL COMMUNITIES

A Virtual Community is a **Digital Social Network** where the users interact online but do not interact (and perhaps do not even know each other) offline. This can include organised groups on **Social Media** (like Facebook groups) but the best examples include websites that offer users a virtual environment in which they can create online identities (called **avatars**). These avatars can be completely different from the user's offline identity.

Increasingly, animated graphics or **virtual reality** (**VR**) technology makes participating in a virtual community as socially complex as physical interactions offline. Avatars offer users anonymity or the chance to act out very different social roles.

Virtual Communities can also be text-based. For example, *Facebook* groups can be private and have moderators ('Mods') who control who is or isn't allowed to join the discussion. These groups are often based around lifestyles, hobbies, political persuasions or religion.

AO2 ILLUSTRATION: MMORPGs and WORLD OF WARCRAFT

A MMORPG is a **Massive Multi-Player Online Roleplaying Game**. These are virtual communities where users create avatars inspired by fantasy or science fiction and to explore or compete in a virtual world – often one with monsters to overcome and treasure to capture, giving a loose objective to the social experience.

The most popular MMORPG is **World of Warcraft (WoW)** which was launched in 2004 and in 2020 there were 4.9 million players. Players create fantasy characters and explore the world of Azeroth, interacting with other players or computer-controlled characters.

Players join together in groups called 'guilds' but the guild members might know nothing about each other's offline lives. Players also meet on online forums (a type of **Social Media**) to share their experiences and post up fan art, fiction and videos.

People marry each other's avatars inside the game and conducted online romantic relationships. 16% of male players and 5% of females reported physically dating someone they met in a MMORPG (**Yee, 2006**).

In 2020, after a scandal involving sexual abuse in the company that created *WoW*, there was an in-game protest conducted by the players' avatars who staged a 'virtual sit-in' outside a tavern in Oribos (a fantasy city in the virtual game world).

World of Warcraft by Blizzard Entertainment

World of Warcraft has spilled over into TV advertising, books, cartoons and a 2016 movie, which is an example of **media convergence**.

RESEARCH PROFILE: NOVECK et al. (2021)

The 2020-21 Covid Pandemic has increased the importance of virtual communities, according to research led by **Beth Simone Noveck**, who carried out interviews with 50 leaders of *Facebook* Groups in 17 countries, along with 26 global experts in online community building. The researchers also ran a YouGov survey of 15,000 Internet users in 15 countries.

77% of respondents indicated that the most important group they're a part of now operates online.

Noveck concludes that DFOC connects people with like-minded people but also facilitates hate groups and dangerous movements. It enables isolated users to feel less alone, leading to strong bonds. There was a link between online communities and meet-ups offline. The Covid Pandemic intensified digital social networks, as people haven't been able to get out and meet with friends and family as they normally would.

Noveck's research is a good example of TRIANGULATION using multiple research methods.

Conclusions About Globalisation & Digital Forms of Communication

The **Digital Revolution** (p27) hasn't just changed the way a bunch of scientists and university students share research – it has gone on to connect the world in new and unexpected ways and become the powerful engine of Globalisation. A **Networked Global Society** (p29) has come into existence, putting the majority of the world's population in instant contact with each other. This new **Global Village** (p28) has far-reaching consequences.

One consequence is that ordinary people greatly increase their **social capital** (p20). Anyone can start amassing *Facebook* friends or *Twitter* followers or start sharing their self-made videos on *YouTube* or *TikTok* and some people have become 'influencers' and media stars by doing this. For other people, these **digital social networks** provide company, emotional support, advice and entertainment.

However, the group that has benefited most from these developments is the group that was already wealthy and powerful to start with. Big businesses have grown bigger, becoming world-straddling **Trans National Corporations (TNCs)** and the big **Tech Companies** have a level of control over our daily lives – for example, to invade our privacy or cut us off from communicating by banning us from their platforms – that goes beyond anything most governments can do.

Marxists have identified the emergence of a new class of global super-rich who are beyond the power of any individual country to control or punish. Most of them make huge profits through using the Internet to their advantage.

Some countries and communities are disturbed by these changes. Digital forms of communication make it very difficult to keep secrets, to control who people speak to or what they see. They open up huge opportunities for criminals and terrorists to carry out their plans on a worldwide scale. They allow deranged and dangerous people who would otherwise be lonely misfits to discover each other and grow more extreme.

One response to this is **cultural defence**, usually in the form of censorship. The **Great Firewall of China** (p13) is one example of a state making sure that Globalisation only happens at the speed and in the way that it decides is best – even though this ignores its citizens' basic freedoms to communicate and learn about the world outside.

Religious fundamentalism is another response which involves trying to 'turn back the clock' and live in the world as it was before Globalisation – perhaps *centuries* before Globalisation.

Even in countries that offer more freedom, people experience anxiety about these developments. Many parents try to limit their children's 'screen time' or use parental settings to limit children's access to adult websites or gambling sites. **Twitter-storms** (p33) erupt and politicians have to respond quickly to the public mood; this is sometimes good for democracy but it can also create a dangerous 'mob mentality' online. Furthermore, the digital network makes it possible to engage in 'cyber-warfare' – such as fears that a country's enemies are interfering with its elections by spreading propaganda and 'fake news' online.

EXAM PRACTICE: DIGITAL FORMS OF COMMUNICATION

The OCR exam has three questions in **Paper 3 Section A**:

Source A	Source B
During the Covid Pandemic, I don't know what I would have done without my online community. Being able to log in and make contact with friendly people, know that they were experiencing the stress and isolation of lockdown, it made all the difference to my mental health. Friends I used to meet in person for a coffee I could now meet online, using Zoom. We moved our weekly pub quiz onto Discord. Lots of Facebook friends became true friends. I feel my social circle has grown as a result and made me stronger too.	Online friends aren't real friends. People chase after 'followers' and 'likes' but the click of a button doesn't show real engagement or concern. The person who cares about you is the person who will drive you to the hospital or house-sit for your dogs. No amount of faceless thumbs-up or heart emojis online adds up to a single meaningful friendship. Anyone logging on looking to feel more connected to other people is chasing an illusion. Your real community is outside your front door: your neighbours.

1. With references to the Source[s], define what sociologists mean by digital social networks. **[9 marks: 5 AO1 + 4 AO2]**

*Make two sociological points about digital networks, one based on Source A and one on Source B. You should quote from the source. It's not vital to refer to named sociologists but you should definitely use some sociological terminology. Then offer examples of networks and make sure each example has an explanation of **why** it is a digital network. For example, "Twitter because you can follow celebrities online and interact with them."*

2. With references to the Source[s], to what extent are digital social networks explained by Postmodernism? **[10 marks: 4 AO1 + 2 AO2 + 4 AO3]**

Write a paragraph about source A then another about source B. Sum up what's in the source and explain what named sociologists would say about it. Then finish off with a brief evaluation (p65) of each view. Make sure you conclude by answering the question (Postmodernism does explain these networks or it doesn't – or perhaps it is just a partial explanation).

3. Evaluate the view that digital forms of communication are becoming more significant in the global world. **[16 marks: 4 AO1 + 4 AO2 + 8 AO3]**

*Write three paragraphs. Each paragraph should introduce a sociological idea with some illustration from the real world. Each paragraph should finish off with developed evaluation (see **Chapter 4** for this). For example, you could write about the Global Village, Media Convergence and a Networked Global Society. Don't forget to answer the question: are digital communications becoming more important or not?*

CHAPTER THREE – IMPACT OF DIGITAL

Digital Forms of Communication (DFOC) have the potential to transform our society – but do they? The 'impact' of DFOC includes changes, for better or worse, in our identities, social inequality and our relationships.

Positive Views of Digital Impact

This is a NEOPHILIAC viewpoint: it sees the **New Media** and DFOC as beneficial for society.

The **Digital Revolution** (p27) has led to a huge increase in **choice**: where you buy your products from, how to pay for things, where to get your news from, what fashions or celebrities to follow, what groups to join and how to interact with people.

Neophiliacs think this choice is **good for the economy**, creating new online business (e-commerce) and new technologies. It is also **good for democracy**. It is easier for people to educate themselves about important matters and play an active role in debate and decision-making, through online petitions or taking part in **Twitter-storms** (p33). The Internet can give a voice to people who previously didn't get heard and it can hold politicians to account by exposing their mistakes and failings. It allows like-minded people to join together and organise protests.

Postmodernists tend to be neophiliacs, although some are aware of the uncertainty and risk involved in the Digital Revolution. **Post-Marxists** (p41) and **4th Wave Feminists** (p24) are neophiles who believe in the power of DFOC to resist Capitalism and challenge privilege.

Negative Views of Digital Impact

This is a CULTURAL PESSIMIST viewpoint. Cultural pessimists believe that the benefits of the **Digital Revolution** have been exaggerated by neophiliacs.

Some cultural pessimists point out that DFOC isn't really something new. Accessing the Internet still requires TV screens, phone lines, etc. People have always signed petitions, written letters of complaint or contributed to the letters pages of newspapers. The only new thing about DFOC is its speed – it offers immediate and constantly changing information, news and entertainment.

A different sort of cultural pessimism argues that the increased choice and interactivity has led to a decline in the quality of **Popular Culture**. There might be more channels for viewers to choose from, but this has led to a dumbing down of content (e.g. endless repeats, reality TV and gambling). This view is particularly associated with **Functionalists** who view DFOC as less authentic than traditional interactions.

Cultural Pessimists also criticise the **polarisation** of online debate – the way DFOC encourages people to adopt extreme positions and not listen to opposing viewpoints, often surrounding themselves with **'echo chambers'** which are digital social networks where everyone you are connected to shares the same opinions as you. They link this to the **Culture Wars** (p45), **Twitter-storms** (p33) and the rise of toxic subcultures like **Incels** (p59).

Regulation of the Internet

The World Wide Web was created by inventors and businesses who were **neophiliacs**, excited about the idea of **free speech** and **free information**. However, many **cultural pessimists** now insist that the Internet is in need of regulation. Even neophiliacs acknowledge that it is easy access to pornography online and free speech is often used to express homophobic, transphobic and racist views and even support violent terrorism.

Regulation would mean setting limits on what can be said or shown online. But what should those limits be and who should police them? One view is that the **'Big Tech' companies** themselves should regulate the Internet. For a long time, the Tech Companies resisted this idea, but they have started taking down offensive material and banning users who post hate speech. For example, since 2017 *Twitter* has been taking down posts that *"harass, intimidate, or use fear to silence another person's voice"* – including the account of former US President Donald Trump.

Another argument is that **state governments** should regulate the Internet and use the law to punish people who incite hate or terror online. Governments have started moving in this direction, which also alarms libertarians who don't want to see free speech become a crime.

Libertarians argue this is unjustified **censorship of free speech**. They are also concerned that regulators are not unbiased and censor some views but not others. However, libertarians tend to be Functionalists or traditional (materialist) Marxists and Feminists; many other groups feel that censorship doesn't go far enough (*c.f.* **Trolls & Incels**, p59). Libertarians illustrate their position by quoting the historian **S.G. Tallentyre (1906)**: *"I disapprove of what you say, but I will defend to the death your right to say it."* In other words, even hateful and violent things should be allowed to be said and not restricted.

RESEARCH PROFILE: CURRAN & SEATON (1991)

James Curran & Jean Seaton argue that patterns of ownership reveal how the news media operate. Capitalism tends to concentrate ownership in fewer and fewer hands and this is happening with the news. This leads to a narrowing of the range of opinions in the news media and a decline in quality and creativity as the Media keeps recycling the most popular things.

Ideally, the news media would reflect the interests of an audience (otherwise they go out business) and it would be easy for anyone to report news themselves on **Social Media**. However, this doesn't happen, because powerful news media companies are perceived as telling 'the truth' rather than just an opinion. **Neophiles** hoped the Internet would bring more points of view into the news media, but Curran & Seaton believe that big news organisations have successfully defended their control: they are an **oligarchy** (a small ruling group). Curran & Seaton point out that national governments limit what news is reported, so state-run news companies (like the BBC) don't offer different views either.

Curran & Seaton believe that the Internet does not represent a break with the past and it does not offer a new environment for ordinary people and marginalised voices to be heard.

PERSPECTIVES ON IMPACT

When it comes to the impact of **Digital Forms of Communication** (**DFOC**) there are a lot of splits within the sociological Perspectives that normally seem to have such united fronts. The good news for students is that this gives you a lot to write about when evaluating different positions.

POSTMODERN PERSPECTIVE: POSTMODERNISM

You would expect **Postmodernists** to be enthusiastic **neophiles** (p38) who view the impact of DFOC as being entirely beneficial. After all, DFOC offers **choice** in a world of **media saturation** and **diversity**. The ability to take on a different identity online links to **fluidity**. Even the multiplying conspiracy theories, Internet hoaxes and fake news online ties in with **Lyotard**'s idea of '**the death of Meta-Narratives**' because there is no longer one 'truth' that everyone accepts.

However, some Postmodernists point out the problems with the uncertainty and confusion this produces. **Zygmunt Bauman (2013)** argues that *"uncertainty is here to stay"* and that in the 21st century each of us needs to *"develop an art of living permanently with uncertainty."* For many people, the pressure to make choices and live without a 'meta-narrative' they believe to be absolutely true creates a stressful sense of uncertainty: are we making the right choices? what is the point of it all? **Lyotard (1979)** calls this state of uncertainty *"the postmodern condition"* and **Bauman** claims we just have to get used to uncertainty as best we can because it's here to stay.

Another troubling idea comes from **Michel Foucault (1926-1984)**, which is that anything that claims to be true is really just a type of language called **discourse**: a sort of 'loaded' way of speaking that society treats as significant and authoritative. Foucault argues that even scientific language is just a discourse: it's only 'true' because society has decided to privilege certain scientists, the things that they say and the way that they say them.

RESEARCH PROFILE: FOUCAULT (1966)

Michel Foucault argues that power is expressed in language and power determines what counts as true and what does not. Foucault argues that *"power is everywhere"* and *"comes from everywhere"* but there are *"regimes of truth"* which means that some language is respected but other language is not. Language affects the way we view the world and causes us to accept things as 'true' or 'false.' Different **discourses** are always battling in society, but none of them is objectively true. Foucault argues that, if you want to change power in society, you need to **deconstruct** the **dominant discourses** that support the *status quo*: show them up for being contradictory or absurd and make them seem unbelievable to people. He calls this '**problematising**' – pointing out the problems with taken-for-granted ideas – and writes:

"Discourse transmits and produces power; it reinforces it, but also undermines and exposes it, renders it fragile and makes it possible to thwart."

Michel Foucault (1926-1984)

It's worth spending a bit longer on Foucault's theory. He imagines society as dominated by ideas coded into language itself. Just by accepting these **discourses** 'at face value' you buy into the ideas in them. Examples including laughing at racist jokes, accepting sexist stereotypes, dismissing some ideas out-of-hand as 'impractical' or 'extremist.' To break free of these limiting forces, you have to **deconstruct** language – expose the faults and contradictions, question everything, turn ideas on their heads and show that things are **problematic**.

Foucault was *not* a Marxist. He recognised that dominant discourses and regimes of truth tended to support dominant groups in society, but he didn't think the dominant groups *deliberately* created these discourses to back up their privileges. He saw it as a two-way process, with language shifting to benefit the dominant groups and groups becoming dominant because of the discourses that support them (think of how the Queen's face on stamps and banknotes supports the British monarchy, but the Queen didn't personally arrange for it to be there).

The Conflict Perspectives have taken aspects of Foucault's theory, creating what has been termed '**Applied Postmodernism**.'

CONFLICT PERSPECTIVE: MARXISM

Foucault's ideas about **discourses** and **deconstruction** don't appeal to traditional (materialist) **Marxists**, who view power as coming from control over **the means of production**, not language. Marxists have a related concept called **ideology** which is different from Foucault's discourse because ideology is an outright lie being presented as truth (e.g. that the ruling classes are doing things in everyone's best interest) whereas Foucault argues 'truth' is only *whatever discourse happens to have the most power at any given time*.

Despite this difference, some **Neo-Marxists** in the 1980s adopted Foucault's ideas and created **Post-Marxism**. Post-Marxists argue that, since society is dominated by a Hegemony (a group of powerful interests that **manufactures consent** through the Media), then most language will be **hegemonic discourse** – language that backs up hegemonic privileges. Post-Marxists see it as their mission to **deconstruct hegemonic discourse** and destroy its power by showing it up for what it is. This leads to a policy of policing language and 'calling out' hegemonic discourse (for example, people sharing racist jokes or using stereotypes about the poor or using words like 'cripple' to refer to people with disabilities).

It suggests that decolonising Western culture means questioning linguistic uses of 'white' and 'black' (e.g. giving someone a 'black mark') and deconstructing popular TV shows, films and everyday behaviours – such as the bias in school curriculums that focus on European history, geography and literature.

Post-Marxists believe that bringing about changes in the way people use language will bring about changes in the way people view society – ultimately, it will lead to people rejecting Capitalism and inequality. **Materialist Marxists** are sceptical about whether meaningful change can happen by focusing on language rather than changing material realities like money and work.

The difference between **Post-Marxism** and **Postmodernism** is that Foucault thought it was impossible to know the truth about reality, but he urged people to deconstruct dominant discourses in a spirit of playful mischief. Post-Marxists use deconstruction more seriously to undermine Capitalism; this is why it can be considered 'Applied Postmodernism.'

RESEARCH PROFILE: LACLAU & MOUFFE (1985)

Ernesto Laclau & Chantal Mouffe developed Post-Marxism with their book *Hegemony & Socialist Strategy* (1985). They reject some very traditional Marxist ideas, like everything in society boiling down to the conflict between the working class and ruling class and defining power as control of the economic means of production. They also reject the idea that Capitalism must inevitably collapse. These ideas are essential to traditional (Materialist) Marxism, so rejecting them is a major break with the past.

Laclau & Mouffe focus instead on **hegemony**: the way privileged people in society are motivated to keep things the way they are and persuade everyone else to go along with them. Instead of focusing entirely on **social class**, they look at how people can be marginalised (denied privileges) because of their race, ethnicity, sexuality or other **aspects of Identity**. They suggest that marginalised people need a discourse that enables them to **resist hegemonic control** and articulate their oppressed situation.

Laclau & Mouffe argue that Post-Marxists need to focus on '**antagonism**' (a point of conflict) to mobilise people – antagonisms could include the environment, LGBT rights or antiracism instead of the working class vs ruling class antagonism. Post-Marxists claim there is a need to challenge dominant discourses about these ideas and develop new discourses that demand **social change**.

CONFLICT PERSPECTIVE: FEMINISM

Foucault's ideas about **discourses** and **deconstruction** don't appeal to traditional (materialist) Feminists either. 2nd Wave Feminists were well aware of sexist language and assumptions, but they focused on winning economic and biological equality for women, rather than trying to redefine things. They recognised **gender roles** as a **social construct** that oppressed women but they saw these roles as being passed on through **socialisation** and **social control**, not language.

3rd Wave Feminists in the 1990s started incorporating Foucault's ideas, starting with **Queer Theory**. Queer Theory focuses on gender behaviour that doesn't fit into the binary of masculine/feminine, such as Gay Subcultures, Drag Subcultures and Trans Identities. This **deconstructs gender discourses**, showing that there are lots of other ways of living and behaving outside of the **dominant discourse** of masculine/feminine.

4th Wave Feminists goes further than this, proposing **gender fluidity**: there are dozens, perhaps hundreds, of Gender Identities on a spectrum and a person might change from one to another. Even biological sex, which was assumed in the past to be a binary (male/female) is reinterpreted as a spectrum and a Trans person might change their sex that was assigned at birth rather than just changing their Gender Identity.

4th Wave Feminists believe that bringing about changes in the way people use language will bring about changes in the way people view sex and gender – it undermines the discourse that gives power to males/masculine and marginalises other sexes and genders; this is why it can be considered '**Applied Postmodernism**.'

These ideas can be termed **Gender Identity Theory**: gender is each individual's lived experience and is a spectrum, not a binary. There are dozens of genders, not just two (some say 57, 63 or 100). As well as masculine and feminine, there is transmasculine, transfeminine, genderqueer, demigirl, demiboy, agender, androgyne, neutrois, pangender, polygender and many more.

Some Gender Identity Theorists go further, arguing that sex itself is a social construct. According to this view, people are **assigned** a binary sex at birth (male or female) but, in reality, sex is no different from Gender Identity and your Gender Identity might turn out to be different from your assigned sex. This idea is essential to current campaigns for the rights of Trans people.

As with Marxism, this argument owes a lot to the influence of Postmodernism, especially Lyotard's idea that no scientific theory can be objectively true or account for the experiences of everyone. Instead, people are radically individual and subjective.

Gender Identity Theory has led to conflicts between Materialist Feminists (who oppose the idea of gender but believe in biological womanhood) and 3rd and 4th Wave Feminists (who embrace the idea of multiple genders as essential to Identity). Materialist Feminists sometimes term themselves **Gender Critical Feminists**, but their critics call them **TERFs** (**Trans-Excluding Radical Feminists**) and accuse their views of being Hate Speech. This battle plays out online, especially on the *Mumsnet* website (p53).

RESEARCH PROFILE: BUTLER (1990)

Judith Butler is a LGBT activist and **Feminist** who wrote the deeply influential book *Gender Trouble* (1990).

Butler focuses on how both gender *and* sex are socially constructed – an idea that was still controversial among 3rd Wave Feminists but has become much more accepted among **4th Wave Feminists**. Butler argues that 'woman' is not a category of people but is **performative**. Womanhood is not something you *are*, it is something you *do*. By **performing** gendered behaviour (e.g. in the way we dress or work) or gendered speech (the way we talk), we construct a **gendered reality** around ourselves.

Judith Butler (photo: Andrew Rusk)

This is similar to **Foucault's idea of discourses** but it includes physical behaviour as well as language and imagery.

Butler recommends **deconstructing hegemonic gender performances**, for example by focusing on 'queer' appearance and behaviour that doesn't fit in the standard categories. Butler singles out **Drag Subculture** as something that makes audiences realise that sex is fluid and gender is a performance. Butler views the standard categories of male/masculine and female/feminine as oppressive and sees queerness as something that liberates people.

4th Wave Feminists use **deconstruction** to undermine the **dominant discourse** about sex and gender. However, **Materialist Feminists** are sceptical about whether any meaningful change can happen by focusing on language rather than changing material realities for women, like money, the law and work (i.e. Patriarchy in offline society). They also criticise 4th Wave Feminism (and **Judith Butler**) for abandoning a strictly biological definition of 'woman.'

Research: go back over your notes from **1A: Socialisation, Culture & Identity** and update ideas about **Gender Identity** in the light of these theories

*The debate within feminism over gender gets pretty intense and sometimes turns hostile, especially online. See the article on **Mumsnet** for more details (p53).*

DIGITAL IMPACT: A TOOLKIT

The OCR Specification asks candidates to reflect on the impact (both positive and negative) of **Digital Forms of Communication** (**DFOC**) and to do so in a global context.

IMPACT ON CULTURE: CONFLICT & CHANGE

Postmodernists argue that Global Culture has come into existence and is going through rapid changes. Change is stressful for people. **Bauman (2013)** argues that people have to live with **uncertainty** now (p40); even though he is not a Postmodernist, **Giddens (1999)** argues that people experience **de-traditionalisation** and have to live with **manufactured risk** (p9).

AO2 ILLUSTRATION: THE CULTURE WARS & 'WOKE'

The **Culture Wars** refers to a conflict across society, but particularly one that plays out in the Media and through DFOC, between two broad groups of people:

Progressives are optimistic about change, uninterested in tradition (including National Identity), opposed to religion and supportive of **Conflict Perspectives** generally. They likely voted against Brexit, wholeheartedly support LGBT rights and oppose racism; in the USA they support abortion but oppose gun ownership. They often support the removal of statues or images that cause offence and generally support **Social Justice** (the reordering of society to give power to previously marginalised groups and remove privileges from dominant groups, p52).

Traditionalists are pessimistic about change but see value in tradition (including National Identity); they see the positive side in religion and are more likely to be religious. They support the **Functionalist** Perspective generally. They likely voted for Brexit, they are cautious in their support for LGBT and antiracism and might oppose these movements; in the USA they are anti-abortion but pro-gun. They are offended by the removal of historic statues and images and alert to the destructive side of the **Social Justice** Movement.

The two sides in this 'war' have trouble sympathising with each other. Online progressives are often given the sarcastic name '**Social Justice Warriors**' (or **SJWs**). They are also identified as '**woke**' (because they are 'awake' to the problems in society and the need for change). Online traditionalists are sometimes called '**Neocons**' (because of a political philosophy called Neoconservatism which supports similar causes). They are also accused of being part of the '**Alt-Right**' which is a US-based online movement that supports nationalism and racism.

It is claimed **Digital Social Networks** produce 'bubbles' or '**echo chambers**' where people only encounter like-minded views which leads to polarisation (getting more extreme and inflexible). '**Cancel Culture**' is where people are silenced during **Twitter-storms** (p33), by **Trolling** (p59) or the closing of venues to prevent them speaking. Online complaints can lead to people being banned from **Social Media** (p39) or even losing their jobs. However, critics claim that concerns about the rise of Cancel Culture is just a **moral panic** aimed at discrediting **Social Justice**.

RESEARCH PROFILE: DUFFY (2021)

Bobby Duffy, director of the Policy Institute, conducted a survey of 2834 UK adults in 2020, weighting the results by age, gender, ethnicity, class, education and family type. He discovered there are not two 'tribes' in the Culture Wars, but rather four:

Traditionalists
Oldest and most heavily male group. Most nostalgic for country's past and proud of British empire. 97% think political correctness gone too far, and most likely to feel UK has done enough on equal rights for historically marginalised groups.

Progressives
Youngest group, with highest education level. Most likely to think women's rights, ethnic minority rights and trans rights not gone far enough. Most likely to be ashamed of British empire, and most in favour of political correctness.

The Disengaged
Stand out for neutrality on politics and Brexit. Least likely to take a position on equal rights for women and ethnic minorities, and least likely to take stance on culture war issues.

Moderates
Support greater rights for women and ethnic minorities – but less strongly than Progressives. Agree political correctness gone too far, yet not nostalgic for past nor proud of empire.

Pie chart values: 26%, 23%, 18%, 32%

Image: The Policy Institute

The Traditionalists are the only group with a male majority (61%) and the only group opposed to the **Black Lives Matter** movement. Progressives are the youngest group, the most ethnically diverse and over half have university degrees.

Although Moderates are the largest group, online they are 'drowned out' by the more active Progressives/Traditionalists. Which way Moderates shift will have a big effect on society.

Duffy & Hewlett (2021) propose that the Culture Wars are an American phenomenon that is being exported to Britain and other countries through **Networked Global Society** (p29) and **Global Culture**. If we follow the American path, these groups in society will become more hostile and extreme.

You can link these findings to **Goodhart**'s idea of the 'Somewheres' vs the 'Anywheres' (p15) and also to **Laclau & Mouffe**'s idea that **Post-Marxism** needs to focus on new 'antagonisms' (p42) to mobilise the Moderates and the Disengaged.

Research: political correctness, the Culture Wars in the USA, more about Social Justice and 'Woke,' recent culture wars over statue toppling, pronouns, the Royal Family, Hollywood movies and TV shows (e.g. *Friends*)

IMPACT ON CULTURE: CULTURAL HOMOGENISATION

An alternative view is that the rise of the Internet accelerates a trend towards **homogenisation** – which means **the tendency for things to become more similar**. This means that people are becoming more similar in their views, tastes, lifestyle and behaviour: they wear the same brands, eat the same food, watch the same shows and have the same outlook. The homogenous culture that everyone is adopting is described as a Western, Capitalist culture – or more specifically an American culture.

The opposite is **cultural heterogenisation** – which means the tendency for society to become more **multicultural** and diverse.

This links to **Giddens (1990**, p9**)** who claims that a Cosmopolitan outlook is emerging that is tolerant and individualistic – although **Giddens (2017)** warns that we might face a *"Cosmopolitan overload"* and a return to traditional thinking (nationalism, religious fundamentalism).

This leads to two questions: (1) **is cultural homogenisation actually happening?** (2) **is that a good thing or a bad thing?**

Homogenous culture might be a good thing if it brought people together, gave them less to fight over, reduced misunderstandings and suspicion and enabled people to travel and mix more easily. However, it would be a bad thing if it led to local cultures being extinguished, religions and languages dying out and the replacement of interesting and meaningful traditions with a bland and shallow **Consumer Culture** that leaves everyone unfulfilled.

Conflict sociologists are particularly concerns that the ***problems*** of Western culture will be exported to the rest of the world, spreading inequality, racism, sexism and exploitation. Other sociologists argue that Western culture can export the ***solutions*** to these problems: human rights, Black Lives Matter, Feminism and democracy.

McDonald's in Osaka, Japan

AO2 ILLUSTRATION: McDONALD'S

McDonald's is a fast food restaurant chain founded by two brothers, Dick and Mac McDonald, in 1940. There are now 36,000 restaurants in 100 countries serving 69 million customers. It delivers a standardised menu (e.g. the Big Mac burger) within a standardised architectural space (the iconic 'Golden Arches' and mansard-style roof, brick walls, Colonial windows).

McDonald's has become a symbol of **Globalisation** and, in 1986, UK campaigners distributed leaflets entitled **'What's wrong with McDonald's — everything they don't want you to know,'** accusing the company of ruining the environment and exploiting workers in developing countries. McDonald's sued them and the trial lasted years. The British court ruled that McDonald's wasn't to blame for deforestation or starvation but had deliberately depressed wages in the food industry.

Super Size Me (2004, dir. Morgan Spurlock) is a documentary film in which Spurlock lived on nothing but McDonald's food for a month; he gained 18 pounds and became depressed. McDonald's later removed the 'supersize' option from the menu, triggering a shift towards clean eating and healthier fast food. This shows Globalisation promoting an unhealthy fast food culture – but also Global Media challenging that culture, leading to reform.

RESEARCH PROFILE: FRIEDMAN (1999)

Thomas Friedman wrote about Globalisation in **The Lexus & the Olive Tree (1999)**; the Lexus motor car symbolises the drive for prosperity and the olive tree symbolises the love of tradition. In one chapter, Friedman argues for the benefits of Globalisation, stating that no country with a McDonald's in it has gone to war with another country with a McDonalds in it. This is jokingly referred to as '**the Golden Arches Theory of Conflict Prevention.**'

Friedman's theory is that a country must reach a certain level of economic development with a large middle class before McDonald's will set up a network of restaurants there. Countries that reach this level become '**McDonald's countries'** and are no longer motivated to fight wars with their neighbours because they can trade instead.

This is part of a wider argument that Globalisation creates economic ties between countries that make it not worthwhile fighting wars.

There are counter examples to Friedman's theory, not least that, soon after his book was published, NATO bombed Yugoslavia and a mob in Belgrade demolished the McDonald's restaurants there. Similarly in 1999, India and Pakistan fought a war over Kashmir and more recently in 2022 Russia invaded Ukraine.

Friedman admits his theory was "*slightly tongue-in-cheek*" but has updated it with the Dell Theory, pointing out that countries don't go to war if they are both part of the Dell Computers supply chain – because this shows a level of economy connection that makes war irrational.

IMPACT ON CULTURE: CULTURAL DEFENCE (GLOCALISATION)

Cultural Defence is a response to Globalisation. It involves 'doubling down' on features that make your own culture distinctive and intensifying them, while rejecting elements of **Global Culture** that are seen as a threat. **Giddens (1990)** points out that religious **fundamentalism** is a type of Cultural Defence (p9): people who are disturbed by **de-traditionalisation** place a much stronger emphasis on their religious traditions than previously and view the encroaching Global Culture as 'unholy' or 'blasphemous.'

Other types of Cultural Defence include insistence on speaking (and making sure your children speak) your native language, wearing traditional clothes, preserving traditional gender roles (such as making sure wives and daughters stay at home) and preserving traditional crafts. You will notice that Cultural Defence can be good or bad. **National Identity** can be part of Cultural Defence, with people becoming more nationalistic in the face of foreign influences.

One way of overcoming Cultural Defence is a strategy known as **glocalisation**, combining Globalisation with local culture. Companies do this to make their products seem less 'foreign' and threatening, for example Domino's succeeded in India by using regional recipes in its pizzas, such as green bananas with chiles, and Nike's 'Year of the Rat' sneakers were popular in China.

A positive view of glocalisation is that it is a sensitive balance of Global Culture while observing local traditions. A more negative view is that it manipulates consumers by offering something superficially familiar in order to make profits for big Capitalist companies.

*This is similar to the debate about Hybrid Culture vs Cultural Appropriation you encountered in **1A: Socialisation, Culture & Identity**.*

Chicken Maharaja Burger (source: McDonald's)

AO2 ILLUSTRATION: McDONALD'S continued

Although McDonald's has a standardised architecture and menu worldwide, it does vary its menu to allow for local traditions. In Japan, there is a **Teriyaki Mac Burger** which is a "*juicy pork burger with a garlicky Teriyaki glaze, lemon sauce and lettuce.*" In India, where beef is unpopular with some Hindus and pork is unclean for Muslims, there is a **Chicken Maharaja Mac**. There are **Coconut Pies** in Singapore, Taro Pies in China (taro is a sweet vegetable that is bright purple), a **McFalafel** in Israel, the **McLobster** in Canada, the **McBeer** in Germany (where McDonald's sells alcohol) and the **Bacon Roll** here in the UK.

This **glocalisation** goes back to the early years of McDonald's and explains the **Filet-O-Fish**. This was the first non-hamburger added to the menu in 1963 and was created by a McDonald's restaurant owner named Lou Groen who struggled to sell meat meals to his Catholic customers on Fridays. Adding a 'fish burger' to the menu brought these customers in and it has remained on the menu since. Despite being horrible.

RESEARCH PROFILE: RITZER (1993)

George Ritzer coined the term '**McDonaldisation**' in his book *The McDonaldization of Society* (1993). He builds on **Max Weber**'s idea that society is becoming more rationalist and scientific.

Being American, he also spells McDonaldization the US way – with a z.

Ritzer argues that the organisation of a McDonald's restaurant reflects the organisation of modern society: (1) **Efficiency:** tasks are done as quickly as possible with minimum waste – the fast food experience where your meal comes pre-packaged; (2) **Calculability:** there is a focus on what can be counted (cost, calories, fat content) rather than incalculable things like quality, taste, enjoyment; (3) **Predictability:** a standardised procedure in the kitchen means that every burger comes out identical; (4) **Control:** CCTVs and other devices monitor the staff or employ technology (like touch screen menus) to do away with human staff altogether.

This leads to unskilled workforces who are underpaid for their work, which is boring and repetitive: this work has been termed a '**McJob**.'

McDonaldisation creeps into other aspects of life (like ordering your taxi using an app, online shopping, drive-thru restaurants, self-service tills in supermarkets, microwavable meals, food full of additives and preservatives, online tuition, speed cameras, etc.).

There is also a reaction *against* this soulless system. **De-McDonaldisation** is a type of Cultural Defence that focuses on products that are authentic, traditional crafts, handmade designs and 'artisanal' products with the human touch. For example, many communities protest at the opening of a Starbucks, believing it will close down local tea shops and cafes.

Research: McJobs, protests against Starbucks, complaints about McDonalds; watch *Super Size Me*

IMPACT ON IDENTITY

Identity is introduced in **1A: Socialisation, Culture & Identity** as a person's self-image, brought about through **socialisation**. The **Interactionist Perspective** also suggests that Identity is shaped by ongoing social interactions. **Becker (1963)** proposes **Labelling Theory** to explain how society labels us based on our behaviour and we either negotiate or internalise these labels, leading to the **Self-Fulfilling Prophecy** where we become the thing we were labelled as.

You were also introduced to **Intersectionality**, which proposes that some Identities are privileged but others are **oppressed** or **marginalised**. **Crenshaw (1991)** shows how marginalised Identities intersect for Black women, creating distinctive patterns of oppression which non-women and non-Blacks fail to appreciate.

3rd **Wave Feminism** and **Neo-Marxism** both incorporate these ideas. **McIntosh (1989)** introduced the phrase '**White Privilege'** and Conflict sociologists propose there are many **hegemonic Identities** (White, male, straight, cis, middle class, able-bodied) which enjoy privileges in society that the privileged people do not recognise.

Foucault (1966, p40**)** adds to this the idea of discourses in society which confer power upon some people and he calls for these discourses to be **deconstructed** (exposed) and **problematised** (dismantled). **Butler (1990)** echoes this idea, calling for the *queer*-ing of masculine and heteronormative values in society (p44).

Digital Forms of Communication (DFOC) have an impact on Identity, either by encouraging Identity to become more fluid or by reinforcing socially normative Identities.

IMPACT ON IDENTITY: SOCIAL CLASS

Class Identity is introduced in **1A: Socialisation, Culture & Identity**, with the three-tier class system of working classes doing manual work, educated middle classes doing office work and the ruling classes inheriting their wealth. **Savage et al. (2013)** conducted the **Great British Class Survey** and added more classes, like the New Affluent Workers and the struggling Precariat.

Social class is judged by others based on factors like the way you dress and especially the way you talk. In the UK, accent is a very strong indicator of class and working class people used to take elocution lessons to adopt a more middle class manner that would give them opportunities.

DFOC removes these class indicators, because communicating through text doesn't reveal accent and the casual conventions of text-speak (and use of emojis) removes indicators of educational level too. Online identities can have a new name and an avatar instead of a personal photograph – and even digital images are easily manipulated to make a person seem more glamorous. This ought to have a **levelling effect** (making everyone on the same level).

AO2 ILLUSTRATION: ONLINE ACTIVISM & SOCIAL JUSTICE

Online activism is working to bring about political change using DFOC. 'Activism' can mean a range of things, from opposing racism to supporting it. **Social Justice** is a particular type of political activism that opposes discrimination and seeks a fairer society.

Social Justice involves (1) fighting for **human rights**; (2) demanding **access** (food, housing, healthcare, education) for marginalised groups; (3) encouraging **participation** – making sure the voices of marginalised groups are heard; (4) demanding **equity** [see below].

Equity is the most controversial aspect of Social Justice. It is not the same as 'equality.' Equality involves making sure everyone gets the same things but equity is making sure people get what they need – that involves giving special help to the most marginalised people but not giving that same help to people who are already privileged. It is sometimes called **'positive discrimination'** (or **'affirmative action'** in the USA) since it involves discriminating in favour of marginalised groups. For example, making sure universities offer more places to students from working class or ethnic minority backgrounds.

*You should be able to see that Social Justice is linked to **Intersectionality** (p23) and forms part of the **Culture Wars** (p45).*

RESEARCH PROFILE: TUFECKI (2017)

Zeynap Tufecki is a Turkish sociologist who wrote *Twitter & Tear Gas* (2017) in which she analyses the link between online activism and public protest. She draws on her own experience of the **2011 'Arab Spring'** when protestors in Africa and the Middle East rose up against their regimes, demanding more freedom and justice for the poor. She also explores the **2011 Occupy Wall Street (OWS)** movement in New York which campaigned against Capitalism, the **2013 Gezi Park protests** for greater freedom in Turkey and the **Black Lives Matter** movement.

Tufecki points out these online movements are **decentralised** (leaderless, not organised) and this enables them to spring into action very quickly but suffer **'tactical freezes'** – they cannot change strategy or negotiate demands: *"Older movements had to build their organizing capacity first, modern networked movements can scale up quickly … without building any substantial organizational capacity before the first protest or march."*

A different explanation of the failure of online activism to achieve political goals is offered by **Evgeny Morozov (2011)** who blames **'slactivism'** – online activism involves clicking likes or texting support, which makes the activist feel good but involves no real commitment.

Research: Arab Spring, Occupy Wall Street (and other Occupy movements, e.g. in London), Gezi Park, Black Lives Matter (e.g. Ferguson protests, George Floyd's murder), Extinction Rebellion, the 2018-19 Yellow Vest protests in France, the 2019-20 Hong Kong protests

IMPACT ON IDENTITY: GENDER

Gender Identity is introduced in **1A: Socialisation, Culture & Identity**, with the idea that **sex** is **binary** (male and female) and biological but **gender** (what is considered masculine and feminine behaviour) is a **social construct**. Traditional (materialist) **Feminism** sees gender as an oppressive construct, forcing women into subordinate roles and justifying male privilege and power.

Many **3rd** and **4th Wave Feminists** reject this analysis. Instead, they view gender as a **spectrum**, allowing for many gender identities. Extreme forms of this **Gender Identity Theory** view sex as a spectrum too. Materialist Feminists (who term themselves as **Gender Critical**) criticise this for removing what defines a woman – her biology. Supporters argue that Gender Identity Theory is important for achieving **Social Justice** (p52) for non-binary women and Trans women and they criticise Gender Critical Feminists as being **TERFs** (**Trans-Excluding Radical Feminists**).

Gender Identity Theory is particularly popular in **online activism**, because DFOC makes it easy for a person to identify differently from how they are perceived to be in their offline life.

AO2 ILLUSTRATION: MUMSNET CONTROVERSIES

Mumsnet is a **Virtual Community** (p34) and a vertical **Social Media** platform (p33), bringing together women and parents for discussion, support and activism. It was founded in 2000 by **Justine Roberts** and has become very influential – before UK elections, political leaders are often interviewed on *Mumsnet* and it has led campaigns for children with disabilities and care after miscarriages. It has 4.3 million users a month, posting over 35,000 messages a day.

Mumsnet is sometimes criticised for contributing to stereotypical ideas about femininity and motherhood. For example, in 2013 the celebrity Amanda Holden was condemned by Mumsnetters for returning to work (on *Britain's Got Talent*) too soon after having a baby.

On the other hand, *Mumsnet* is also a focus for Feminist online activism, but this has led to controversy. *Mumsnet* is criticised for allowing **transphobic** discussion. Journalist **Eve Livingstone** (2018) accuses *Mumsnet* as being *"a toxic hotbed of transphobia"* and companies like *Flora* margarine have boycotted promotions organised by *Mumsnet* because of such allegations. Justine Roberts insists *Mumsnet* is only allowing free speech and debate over Gender Identity, including respecting the views of Gender Critical Feminists.

RESEARCH PROFILE: HARAWAY (1985)

Donna Haraway wrote *A Cyborg Manifesto* **(1985)** arguing for the positive role that science and technology can have for female Identity. Haraway's *Manifesto* pre-dates the invention of the World Wide Web but it is way ahead of its time.

Haraway argues against **essentialism** – the idea that there is anything that absolutely defines what it is to be a woman. This is an insight that was taken up by **3rd** and **4th Wave Feminists** and Gender Identity Theory. She regards language itself as 'coded' with patriarchal meanings which women need to break free from; this is similar to **Foucault**'s discourses (p40) and the Queer Theory of **Judith Butler** (p44).

She uses the Science Fiction idea of a **cyborg** – a creature part human, part machine – to describe how a woman could leave gender behind and why Feminism should bring together different Identities under its cause. This insight was taken up by **Intersectionality** and is similar to **Laclau & Mouffe**'s recommendations for **Post-Marxism** (p42).

Haraway's cyborg seems to be an imaginative metaphor for combining and changing Identities – she's not *literally* claiming women should turn themselves into machines! However, the **Digital Revolution** (p27) has given a new meaning to her ideas. **Amber Case (2007)** argues that DFOC enables people to express themselves through machines (computers) and that **Virtual Communities** (p34) are rather like Haraway's cyborgs, where technology helps people leave their gendered bodies behind and define their own Identities.

Research: the debate over Gender Critical Feminists/TERFS – but be warned, you will come across strong language on both sides

IMPACT ON IDENTITY: AGE

Age Identity is introduced in **1A: Socialisation, Culture & Identity**, with the idea of maturation being a biological change but Age as a social construct, putting people into categories like Child, Youth, Adult, Middle Aged and Elderly. **Postman (1994)** argues that Childhood is disappearing because of new technologies like TV and computers and the new relationships created by DFOC.

Research: review your notes on **Postman**'s *Disappearance of Childhood* from **1A** and apply them to DFOC. If you studied **Youth Subcultures** in **1B**, review your notes on **Maffesoli**'s **Neo-Tribes** and apply that to DFOC too.

Postmodernists think that DFOC have accelerated the **fragmentation** of age groupings that used to be 'written in stone.' Instead, age is a **fluid** Identity: adults (sometimes termed '**kidults**') play online video games or follow movie franchises enjoyed by children (e.g. *Star Wars* or *Harry Potter*), middle aged people listen to pop music and join fan subcultures (e.g. K-Pop or Japanese anime) and elderly people use online dating to enjoy romance and sex.

Critical Perspectives have a similar view about DFOC changing Age Identities. **Marxists** argue that elderly people are discarded by society when they stop contributing to Capitalism by working; **Feminists** argue middle aged women are discarded when the menopause makes them no longer fertile (and therefore no longer desired by men). DFOC allow older people to continue to be socially, economically and politically active.

On the other hand, the Elderly can be a **Digital Underclass** (p60) who are cut off from DFOC because they lack the skills to make use of the Internet.

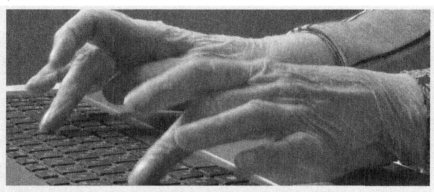

AO2 ILLUSTRATION: GREY POWER & NOSTALGIA

The **Grey Pound** is an expression for the economic power of the Elderly. In the past, the Elderly were referred to as 'pensioners' and seen as poor, but since the **2008 Global Financial Crisis (GFC)** the Elderly have become better-off compared to the young. *Saga*, a company offering leisure products for the Elderly, estimates in 2020 that the Grey Pound is worth £320 billion a year. This increased during the 2020-21 Coronavirus Pandemic as older people embraced DFOC and Internet shopping.

Linked to this is the idea of **Grey Power**: as people live longer but have fewer children, the Elderly become a larger proportion of the population. Moreover, they are the group most likely to vote in elections. This means politicians are under pressure to pass laws that keep the Elderly happy. The politicians themselves tend to be old: Donald Trump was the oldest President to be inaugurated at 70 until Joe Biden replaced him, aged 78.

A motivating factor for many older people is **nostalgia** – a sentimental and affectionate view of the past. The political influence of nostalgia could explain the 2016 election of Donald Trump ('Make American Great Again') and the Brexit Referendum result, a result that politician **Vince Cable (2018)** blamed on *"nostalgia for a world where passports were blue, faces were white and the map was coloured imperial pink."*

Capitalism exploits nostalgia in its advertising: TV ads featuring *Top Cat* and the *Flintstones*, *Adidas* re-releasing *Superstars* and *Gazelle* trainers or the success of *Pokémon Go* in 2016. If society is dominated by **uncertainty** (p40) and risk (p9), then nostalgia is an important source of security for a growing number of people.

RESEARCH PROFILE: PAGE (2019)

Ben Page is the head of the survey company Ipsos Mori who collaborated with the Centre for Ageing Better to produce *The Perennials: the future of ageing* (**2019**). 'Perennial' is a term coined to mean the opposite of the youthful Millennials born in the 1980s and '90s.

Page cites an Ipso Mori **Global Trends Survey** which found 49% of UK respondents would like their country to be 'the way it used to be' but this rose to 58% for the over-60s.

The survey also found that on average 'Old Age' starts at 74 in Spain but 55 in Saudi Arabia, 61 for the under 24s but 72 for the over-55s. This shows the **social construction** of Age Identity. The report agrees that older people are 'airbrushed' out of the Media: only 1.5% of TV characters are Elderly and most have minor roles.

The report concludes that despite negative stereotypes of ageing, old age is becoming a time of opportunity for many people.

Research: more examples of nostalgia in advertising; the *Friends* reunion; bands doing comeback tours; nostalgia music and TV channels

IMPACT ON INEQUALITY

Inequality is introduced in **2B: Understanding Social Inequalities** as a person's life chances that can be improved by work, wealth and education or held back by discrimination or lack of opportunity. **Meritocracy** is an understanding that society is structured to reward talent and hard work, but **Bourdieu (1984)** argues that society is structured around **Social Reproduction**, ensuring that inequalities are reproduced from one generation to the next.

Marxists identify the root cause of this inequality in **Capitalism**. Many **Feminists** would agree but insist that women are subject to even greater inequality, since they are subordinate to men in a **Patriarchal** society.

Intersectionality proposes that some Identities are privileged but others are **oppressed** or **marginalised**. Critical theories explain inequalities through this intersection of oppression for some people and **unearned privilege** for others.

Applied Postmodernism (e.g. **Post-Marxism** and **3rd** or **4th Wave Feminism**) identifies the source of oppression in language itself. It calls for **deconstructing**, **problematising** or *queer*-ing the taken-for-granted assumptions in language to draw attention to inequality and demolish the justifications for it.

Digital Forms of Communication (DFOC) have an impact on Identity, either by encouraging Identity to become more fluid or by reinforcing socially normative Identities.

IMPACT ON INEQUALITY: SOCIAL CLASS

DFOC allows people to educate themselves, find work, find good deals on purchases or get help with problems. People without wealth or **Social Capital** (p20) can promote themselves online, gather followers and acquire influence. This should be **empowering** the working classes.

On the other hand, access to **Digital Social Networks** requires money (for computers, tablets or smartphones as well as broadband access) and skills. This leads to a **Digital Divide** between people with the technology and skills to benefit from DFOC and those without. Moreover, Capitalist businesses use DFOC to exploit working class people. Online gambling was worth £5.7 billion in the UK in 2020 and people from deprived backgrounds spend more on 'virtual slot machines' that are particularly addictive (source: the **Gambling Commission**).

AO2 ILLUSTRATION: UBER & THE GIG ECONOMY

Uber is a US Tech company founded in 2009 whose mobile app puts customers in touch with taxi drivers or food delivery firms. Uber takes a 25% cut for the service. It is the largest company operating in the '**gig economy**.' The gig economy is an arrangement where people work flexible hours providing on-demand services, with DFOC putting them in touch with customers or employers. Tech companies make a profit from each transaction. For employers, the gig economy lets them hire workers for single tasks (like a digital artist or delivery drivers) without taking them on as a full-time employee. For customers, it means a worker (like a taxi driver) can be hired quickly at low cost.

The gig economy means workers can get work quickly and only work the hours they choose to work. However, gig workers don't get the holidays, pensions, sickness benefits and other legal protections that full-time workers do, even if they work full-time hours.

Critics claim that the gig economy exploits the poorest workers, giving them no rights and forcing them to work long hours to support themselves. Uber claims it is just a booking agent and the taxi drivers are all self-employed. However, in 2021 the **UK Supreme Court** ruled that Uber is in fact an employer and must protect its drivers. Cities like London have tried to ban Uber, to protect the rights of taxi drivers and protect passengers.

Uber in Beijing (photo: bfishadow)

RESEARCH PROFILE: BURGESS (2020)

Gemma Burgess reports on an ongoing research project into the digital divide carried out by **Cambridge University**. She argues that the divide has been worsened by the 2020-21 Coronavirus Pandemic. Burgess points out the using DFOC requires a range of **digital skills** (communication by text, using search engines, buying or downloading from the World Wide Web, problem solving, staying safe online) as well as access to expensive technology. She concludes that **digital exclusion** affects a fifth of the UK population, with 8% of people having zero digital skills and 12% being limited in digital skills. Of the 8 million people in the UK without access to the Internet, 90% are economically deprived.

The Covid Pandemic increased the importance of **Digital Social Networks** (working or studying online and staying in contact with friends and family through DFOC), so this has increased the exclusion for 20% of people with limited or no digital skills.

Research: controversies about Uber; the gig economy; problems with online gambling

IMPACT ON INEQUALITY: GENDER

DFOC allows women to study, find work, find good deals on purchases or get help with problems like domestic violence. **Social Media** (p33) provides support for women – such as **Mumsnet** (p53). Online activism raises the awareness of problems facing women, such as the **Everyday Sexism Project** (p24). This should be **empowering** for women.

On the other hand, the Internet can be a hostile place for women. Internet Trolls frequently target women with rape threats. Revenge Porn is used by embittered former partners who upload sexually explicit images relating to women they are angry about. The Internet makes it easier for stalkers to harass women and sex-traffickers to exploit women.

The World Wide Web hosts a lot of pornography and the most visited pornography website, *Pornhub*, gets as much traffic as *Netflix* or *Linkedin*. It is estimated that 1 in 7 web searches is for pornography. A report from **Ofsted (2021)** claims school-age boys collect pornography on their mobile phones and use it for sexual bullying of girls: 9 in 10 school-age girls report sexist bullying and being sent unwanted pornographic images.

Feminists are divided over the issue of pornography. Traditional (materialist) Feminists tend to be anti-porn, viewing it as the exploitation and objectification of women's bodies and linking it to violent and **misogynistic** (women-hating) attitudes in society. However, some 4th Wave Feminists are in favour of **'sex-positive'** pornography that empowers women or *queer*-ing **heteronormative** sexuality (heterosexual, male-centred) through porn.

AO2 ILLUSTRATION: TROLLS, THE MANOSPHERE & INCELS

An Internet 'Troll' is someone who posts messages on **Social Media** (p33) or **Virtual Communities** (p34) to provoke or upset other people, usually to get attention for themselves but sometimes to damage someone's reputation or interfere with politics. The worst Trolling involves very offensive threats, including death threats, and **slurs** (offensive names, often sexist, racist, homophobic or transphobic). Trolling is a type of **cyber-bullying**. Trolling is particularly common on anonymous online forums (like *Reddit* or *4chan*), *Twitter* and anonymous *YouTube* comments.

Misogynist (women-hating) trolling is a growing problem. In 2020, the Australian *Herald Sun* had to close its comments section on women's football coverage because of offensive trolling. According to a **2020 BBC Survey**, 30% of British sportswomen report being trolled on social media, with offensive remarks about their appearance and attractiveness, up from 14% in 2015.   Trolls also target women with rape threats.

Some of this trolling comes from anti-Feminist virtual communities known as the '**manosphere.**' These groups tend to be traditionalists in the **Culture Wars** (p45) and some are **Alt-Right** extremists. **Incels** are an exceptionally misogynistic virtual community regarded by many as a hate group or even as terrorists. Incel stands for 'involuntary celibate' as they blame women for not providing them with sex. Incels go beyond trolling: since 2014 there have been at least 7 mass murders and 56 deaths caused by men who were involved with the Incel movement online.

Research: refer to your notes on **Faludi (1999)** in **1A: Socialisation, Culture & Identity**; is the 'backlash' against Feminism and the misogyny she detected in American men present online?

RESEARCH PROFILE: MOLONEY & LOVE (2018)

Mairead Moloney & Tony Love studied the increase in misogynist trolling in social media. They identify (1) **online sexual harassment**, pestering women for sexual relations (such as sending nude images); (2) **gendertrolling**, which is targeting non-conforming or successful women for trolling; (3) **e-bile**, which is personal abuse and sexual slurs; (4) **disciplinary rhetoric**, meaning death or rape threats to silence women.

Moloney & Love take an **Interactionist** approach, looking at **'Virtual Manhood Acts'** (**VMA**). Manhood Acts are behaviours which **enforce hegemonic gender norms** (i.e. they oppress women and elevate men as well as oppressing anyone falling outside traditional binary ideas of gender). VMA can be textual (writing), verbal (spoken) or visual (images).

They conclude that the same interactions take place online as in the offline world and their purpose is to keep men "in the box." This is the idea that traditional masculinity occupies a 'box' a deviating outside of the box makes a person **effeminate** or **queer**. Men police the borders of the 'box' and use slurs and labels for those outside it (women, LGBT people, disabled people, etc.). Online fluid identities make it harder to keep men "in the box" which explains the hostility and aggression on VMA towards women.

IMPACT ON INEQUALITY: AGE

DFOC allows older people to shop, seek relationships or get help with problems. DFOC allows people who are no longer economically active to promote themselves online, gather followers and acquire influence. This should be **empowering** the Elderly.

On the other hand, access to **Digital Social Networks** requires skills the Elderly often lack. They have been termed a **Digital Underclass** – as opposed to the young who grew up after the **Digital Revolution** (p27) who are **Digital Natives**. For example, 99% of adults (aged 16-34) use the Internet at least once every three months, but this was only 54% for those aged 75+ (source: **ONS, 2019**). However, this was an increase from only 20% of 75+ people in 2011.

Don't confuse the Digital Underclass with the New Right's idea of the Underclass. The Digital Underclass are people who don't go online – it's nothing to do with single parents on benefits!

AO2 ILLUSTRATION: THE ELDERLY DURING LOCKDOWN

During the **2020-21 Coronavirus Pandemic**, the UK and other countries imposed Lockdowns: people were asked to stay at home and avoid contact with friends, neighbours and family members. This had a big impact on the Elderly who already suffer social isolation (due to family growing up and moving away, peers or partners becoming ill or dying, retirement, etc).

Many people turned to DFOC to stay in touch with family and support groups. Daily users of the video app *Zoom* went from 10 million to 200 million during 2020.

Many older people turned to online shopping to get their groceries without the risk of going to supermarkets. Online shopping by the over-75s increased by 24% after the Lockdowns started (source: **Age UK**). However, Age UK claims this increase in Internet usage has mostly come from existing Internet users going online more often. The shift to online shopping is in fact leaving many older people behind. Age UK trains volunteers to become 'Digital Buddies' for the elderly in their community and help them get online.

RESEARCH PROFILE: HU & QIAN (2021)

Canadian researchers **Yang Hu & Yue Qian** argue that over-60s dependent on online contact felt more lonely during Lockdown. They survey 5148 people aged 60+ in the UK and 1391 in the US, both before and during Lockdown. The increase in loneliness was *higher* for those who reported more virtual contact. This supports a **cultural pessimist** view of DFOC (p38).

The findings only show that virtual contact is *associated* with loneliness - not that it is the cause. People who feel more isolated to start with will make virtual contact more frequently. But it shows that virtual contact on its own is not beneficial to older people's mental health –there is an improvement when online contact is supplemented by face-to-face contact.

IMPACT ON RELATIONSHIPS

The impact of DFOC on relationships illustrates the difference between **neophiles** and **cultural pessimists** (p38).

Neophiles see DFOC as beneficial for our relationships. Through **Digital Social Networks** we can have more relationships, maintain relationships at a distance and have new types of relationships. Examples include video conferencing at work or in education, online dating and the membership of **virtual communities** (e.g. a 'guild' in *World of Warcraft*, p34). They see these online relationships as just as valuable, productive and satisfying as face-to-face relationships.

Cultural Pessimists see DFOC as unsatisfactory substitutes for 'real' or face-to-face relationships: they are inauthentic, shallow and full of deception and confusion. Pessimists point out that online friends are not really emotionally committed to you and may not be who they claim to be. Your privacy can be hacked and your identity stolen. The **Twitter-storms** (p33) and **Trolling** (p59) that goes on online can be immensely stressful and hurtful. Because of the anonymity online, people can be unrestrained and extreme in their behaviour. **Sherry Turkle (2011)** warns that online relationships make us *"alone together"* (the title of her book, which links to Putnam's *Bowling Alone*, p21) – despite receiving daily emails and chatting online, people become isolated and lonely.

Postmodernists are positive about online relationships, but **Zygmunt Bauman (2013)** is aware of the uncertainty involved in them – but he argues this uncertainty is now a characteristic of *all* our relationships. For example, in the UK 42% of marriages end in divorce (source: **ONS, 2019**).

4th Wave Feminists are also positive about online relationships because of the possibility of defining your own identity and sharing experiences of oppression. For example, **Laura Bates' Everyday Sexism Project** allows women to share their testimonies of harassment, discrimination and abuse. However, the rise of **misogynistic Trolls** and **Incels** (p59) shows that toxic relationships get a boost from the Internet too.

Post-Marxists see the benefits of online relationships to organise **Social Justice** activism (p52) and challenge the **hegemonic discourses** (p41) that shape face-to-face relationships. However, because so much of the Internet is controlled by the big Tech companies and so much online content is created by big Media companies, Capitalist values (advertising, shopping, branding, stereotyping) are very influential online too.

AO2 ILLUSTRATION: ONLINE DATING & TINDER

Organised 'matchmaking' has been around since the 19th century, but online dating began with *Kiss.com* (1994), followed by sites like *Match.com* (1995), *Gaydar* (1999), *eHarmony* (2000) and *Grindr* (2009). These sites use mathematical calculations (algorithms) to match people by their preferences and interests.

Tinder was launched in 2012 and is an app that lets you match yourself with other users by swiping on their profile picture: users who match each other are put into contact.

The popularity of these sites is growing: between 2015-19 32% of new couples met online, an increase from 19% between 2005-14 (source: **Statistia**). *Tinder* hit a record 3 billion swipes on one day in March 2020 and has broken that record hundreds of times since then.

Not all online dating experiences are positive. 57% of female online daters experience harassment (source: **Pew, 2020**). Catfishing is when someone adopts a fake identity to manipulate a dating partner – either to exploit them sexually or cheat them out of money. There can be long-term trauma and depression after being victimised like this.

Three Chechen girls 'catfished' the terror group Islamic State (ISIS) by pretending to be recruited on **Social Media**, giving the recruiters fake names and photographs, taking $3300 to travel to the Middle East, then keeping the money and closing their accounts (source: **RT News, 2015**). No one feels sorry for terror groups who get swindled this way, but it illustrates the potential for deception and exploitation in online dating.

RESEARCH PROFILE: MILLER (2011)

Daniel Miller wrote *Tales From Facebook* (2011) drawing on interviews with *Facebook* users in Trinidad. *Facebook* is the world's largest **Social Media** site which went public in 2006 and has 2.8 billion daily users worldwide (source: **Statistia, 2020**) – although there were 'only' 500 million users when Miller carried out his research.

One is an ageing man who uses Facebook to get over his constraints; another is a young man who finds comfort and a **Virtual Community** in the online game *Farmville*; there is also a Christian who uses *Facebook* to evangelise and stay in touch with other church members.

Miller argues that *Facebook* restores close social relationships that were previously declining and brings people together over great distances. However, he also observes how *Facebook* posts revealed an affair, leading to the break-up of a marriage, and observes the consequences for a music star who has had a sex video leaked – both having effects offline as well as online.

Miller focuses entirely on *Facebook* as a **Digital Social Network** rather than a Capitalist business that makes profits from advertising. **Marxists** would draw attention to the controversies about *Facebook*-users losing their privacy and the company treating them as commodities to advertisers – and sharing data about its users with companies like *Amazon* and *Netflix* (source: **New York Times, 2018**).

Neither does Miller analyse the sexism going on in *Facebook* discourses from a **Feminist** perspective – such as the analysis carried out by **Moloney & Love** (p59).

Conclusions about the Impact of Digital Forms of Communication

Many social scientists (sociologists and psychologists) suspect that **digital forms of communication** don't just let us communicate faster, more easily, with more people – they actually change the way we feel about ourselves and relate to each other.

Neophiles hope that these changes are for the best. They claim that the Internet is making us all more politically engaged. It is easy to get involved in online activism, hard to stay ignorant of crimes and corruption going on in society and the Internet provides a powerful way for protesters to catch the attention of politicians and team up with activists in other countries to create a truly worldwide movement.

Even though Globalisation threatens to make everyone **homogenous** (p47), the Internet enables local communities to band together, assert their identities and preserve their traditions through **cultural defence** (p49). This is particularly true for communities who exist as a diaspora – as a scattering of families spread over many countries due to migration.

Women in particular have used this new technology to empower themselves and raise awareness of how they are mistreated. **4th Wave Feminism** has made full use of the Internet to bring women together and share experiences like everyday sexism and #MeToo. It has also joined with activists from other backgrounds in the **Social Justice** movement (p52) which aims to get equity for marginalised people.

However, not everything is so positive. The sort of engagement people make with online causes is often shallow and temporary – slacktivism, not activism. The blending of local cultures with Global Culture is often a cynical marketing ploy by **Trans National Corporations** (**TNCs**) to sell their products to resisting markets. **Glocalisation** (p49) only happens in ways that suit big businesses.

Moreover, Social Justice isn't the only movement to get empowered online. The Alt-Right is also active on the Internet, with many groups promoting White Supremacy, homophobia and transphobia, as well as religious fundamentalist groups with violent or bigoted agendas. The Internet has no favourites and it empowers the bad as well as the good.

All of this assumes that everyone can actually get online. There is a **Digital Underclass** (p60) of people who cannot afford the modern technology or lack the skills to use it effectively. There are many vulnerable people ready to be exploited online, either by cash-grabbing companies, hoaxes, gambling sites, credit companies or aggressive **Trolls** (p59). Online hate doesn't stay online: it spills onto the streets in mass shootings and bombings. There is also pornography, which is said to make up 35% of all Internet downloads.

It seems the Internet is a mixed blessing because its amazing potential is put to use by people with different agendas as online, as in offline life, the groups with the most money to spend have the biggest influence.

EXAM PRACTICE: IMPACT OF DIGITAL COMMUNICATION

The OCR exam has three questions in **Paper 3 Section A**:

Source A	Source B
Not everyone enjoys the connectedness and fast-paced change of the 21st century. Some see it as a threat to their traditional values and worry that their children will be lured away from their culture by fashion, advertising, video games and travel. One response to this is religious fundamentalism, which rejects the modern world as sinful. However, even fundamentalists use the Internet, to preach their vision of the righteous life, to recruit new members and to condemn the changes that cause them such distress.	There are over 7000 languages in the world, but over half of the population speak just ten – like English, Spanish, Mandarin or Arabic – as their native language. Minority languages are dying out and one 'dies' every week. However, language learning websites and apps are keeping minority languages alive. Online communities promote their language and the culture it expresses, like the Digital Himalayas project, the Diyari blog, the Arctic Languages Vitality project and the Enduring Voices Project.

1. With references to the Source[s], define what sociologists mean by cultural defence. **[9 marks: 5 AO1 + 4 AO2]**

*Make two sociological points about cultural defence, one based on Source A and one on Source B. You should quote from the source. It's not vital to refer to named sociologists but you should definitely use some sociological terminology. Then offer examples of cultural defence and make sure each example has an explanation of **why** it is cultural defence. For example, "Creating an app to teach children your language so your culture won't die out when you pass away."*

2. With references to the Source[s], to what extent do digital forms of communication promote cultural defence? **[10 marks: 4 AO1 + 2 AO2 + 4 AO3]**

Write a paragraph about source A then another about source B. Sum up what's in the source and explain what named sociologists would say about it. Then finish off with a brief evaluation of each view (p65). Make sure you conclude by answering the question (it does promote cultural defence, or it doesn't or perhaps it only partially promotes defence but also undermines it).

3. Evaluate the view that digital forms of communication have a positive impact on people's identities. **[16 marks: 4 AO1 + 4 AO2 + 8 AO3]**

*Write three paragraphs. Each paragraph should introduce a sociological idea with some illustration from the real world. Each paragraph should finish off with developed evaluation (see **Chapter 4** for this). For example, you could write about social class, gender and age as Identities and the impact on each. Don't forget to answer the question: does the Internet have a positive impact or not?*

CHAPTER 4 – EVALUATION

In **Paper 3 Section A (Globalisation & the Digital Social World)**, question 2 assesses **AO3**/evaluation with the phrase *"to what extent?"* while question 3 asks for a developed evaluation (with the command *"evaluate," "assess"* or *"discuss"*).

'To what extent does not have to be developed or address theoretical issues. It can be a common-sense comment. It should be a simple **strength**, **weakness** or **comparison**.

A developed evaluation needs to address theoretical or methodological issues. It needs to go deeper than a 'brief evaluation' and look at an issue from alternative perspectives or work through the implications of a viewpoint.

Here are some evaluative positions candidates can adopt:

Brief Evaluations

These points are suitable for Q2. You can use them in Q3 as well, but their simplicity makes them hard to turn into developed points, so you might miss out on the higher AO3 band marks. Still, better to write something than nothing at all.

"Not all people…" / Over-generalising

Structuralist Perspectives (traditional **Marxism** and **Feminism**) are particularly prone to sweeping generalisations. They often claim that everyone is motivated by the same thing or experiences the same oppression or wants the same outcomes. For example, Marxists claim everyone is part of a social class and Feminists claim all women are in some way oppressed.

To evaluate these ideas, point out that not all people fit into this mould. Not all old people use the Internet (p60), not all women experience abuse online (p59) and not all people benefit from Globalisation (p49**Error! Bookmark not defined.**).

If you are writing about some empirical research, point out that its sample group doesn't resemble everyone. Not all *Facebook*-users are from Trinidad like the ones that Daniel Miller studied (p62).

It's important not to be formulaic. Say *why* not all people are like this: give an example of one of the exceptions. Not all people benefit from Globalisation, *because some people find their traditional values threatened by change*. Not all old people use the Internet *because some don't have the computer skills to get online or use apps*.

"It's out-of-date..." / Time-locked

There's a crucial date in the study of digital forms of communication and it is 2005 – the arrival of **Web2.0** (p27). Can studies from before this – or from before the public availability of Web1.0 in 1991, really tell us anything about digital communication today?

To evaluate these studies, point out that so much has changed. In Web2.0 there is much greater interactivity: users can post up comments on sites, use emojis, upload their own media content, manipulate memes or have instant real-time chat and video communication.

Once again, it's important not to be formulaic. Say **why** one of these changes matters for this particular study: give an example of one of the exceptions. Haraway's idea of Cyborgs (p54**Error! Bookmark not defined.**) is out-of-date because *people meet online where their bodies can't be seen and don't define them*. Putnam's *Bowling Alone* (p21) is out-of-date *because there is online activism now so you don't have to leave your home to get involved in civic activities*.

Online doesn't always reflect offline

Sociologists find lots of links between online and offline behaviour, but there are differences too. The way people behave online and the things they watch and do might not have any effect on their offline behaviour.

To evaluate these ideas, point out that people have a completely different social setting offline and can use body language and facial expressions to communicate. They will also be judged on things like their class, race or gender or their disabilities.

It would be formulaic just to say "people might behave differently offline" and leave it at that. Say **why** the offline behaviour might be different: give an example of one of the influences. For example, online activism might just be slacktivism *because getting involved in protests offline might be time-consuming or even dangerous*.

Developing Evaluations

These points are suitable for Q2 and Q3. Their complexity makes them suitable for turning into developed points, so you can qualify for higher AO3 band marks on Q3.

"It's too Structuralist" / Postmodernist critique

Structuralist Perspectives make sweeping generalisations because they study society as a whole and focus on important institutions rather than individual people. The **Postmodern** Perspective criticises this, saying that in the 21st century people are much more individualistic and construct their Identities from lots of different sources rather than being identified purely by their class, gender or age group.

To evaluate these ideas, point out that a Postmodernist approach might be better. Rather than studying the working class or women or the elderly, study people who have a certain lifestyle in common (like vegans, evangelical Christians or fans of online vloggers).

As usual, avoid being formulaic. Say *why* the Postmodern approach would be better: give an example of one of the benefits. Take a Postmodern approach to studying the Gender, *because instead of just categorising people as male or female you can categorise them by lots of different Gender Identities.*

Development

If you bring in Postmodernism as the solution to the problem, don't stop there. You could give examples of studies that incorporate Postmodern ideas (like **Butler** incorporating discourses into her Queer Theory, p44) or explain how later research incorporates aspects of Postmodernism (like **4**[th] **Wave Feminism** focusing on people with different Gender Identities).

Alternatively, criticise your own improvement: discuss the drawbacks of using the Postmodernist approach (e.g. the ideas are very vague and subjective and hard to back up with evidence, such as Gender Identities that are hard to define clearly).

"This is similar to..." / Comparisons

Sometimes, different sociologists or different Perspectives end up saying similar things, although usually for different reasons Marxists and Feminists both agree there is propaganda and brainwashing (**ideology**) in the news and in schools. Marxists and Postmodernists both agree that Globalisation is stressful and difficult for people.

To evaluate these ideas, point out the similarity between the sociology you are writing about and another Perspective or research study. If you have explained that Marxists think that Globalisation spreads Capitalism around the world, explain that Postmodernists also think we live in a Hyper-Reality made up of media images from global companies.

As usual, don't be formulaic. Say *why* the two approaches are so similar *or* say why they are also different: give an example. Marxists and Postmodernists agree on Globalisation because they both think it changes the way we live and relate to each other, *although Marxists think this is always an alienating and exploiting arrangement* and *Postmodernists focus more on how so much choice creates uncertainty*.

Development

If you think two Perspectives are similar, don't stop there. You could give examples of studies from each perspective, like **Robinson** writing about the transnational bourgeoisie waging war on humanity (p12) compared to **Bauman**'s concept of uncertainty (p40) or explain how later research incorporates both perspectives, like the Post-Marxists using Applied Postmodernism to promote **Social Justice** (p52).

Alternatively, criticise the very similarity you suggested: discuss the how differences between the two approaches are more important than similarities (Marxists recognise the overall social context of Capitalism, whereas Postmodernists see a fluid and fragmented world with no overall meaning).

"A Intersectionalist would say ..." / Intersectional critique

Intersectionality makes a powerful criticism of other Perspectives and especially research from before the 1990s or the 21st century.

Intersectionality proposes that people are privileged or oppressed based on their Identities and the oppressed Identities intersect in ways that intensify the oppression. This is a criticism of Perspectives that view people through a single lens (e.g. just looking at age, or gender, or class).

In order to avoid being formulaic, say *why* an Intersectional approach would be better: give an example of the benefits. Take an Intersectional approach to studying the impact of digital communication, *because it will focus on working class women experience the Internet differently from middle class women – or how older women have different experiences from young women.*

Development

If you think Intersectionality is good, don't stop there. You could give examples of studies from the Intersectionality perspective (like **Butler**'s Queer Theory or **Laclau & Mouffe**'s Post-Marxism, p42) or explain how Intersectionality appears in other perspectives (like how Social Justice's concern for equity combines Intersectionality and Marxism).

Alternatively, criticise the Intersectionality idea you suggested: discuss the flaws with Intersectionality (like the way it draws Feminists' attention away from women and Marxists' focus away from the working class).

"A weakness of this Perspective is …" / Standard theoretical critiques

Marxism

Marxism ignores progress: In the last 200 years, Capitalist societies have abolished slavery, set up human rights, created a welfare state and free education and healthcare for all. Marxists often talk as if this hasn't happened or as if it happened *in spite of* Capitalism. This pessimistic view of the past and the future perhaps exaggerates social injustice. *However* Intersectionality shows us that these benefits have been enjoyed by people with privileged Identities more than marginalised ones and **Social Justice** aims to change that.

Marxism is a conspiracy theory: It's standard for Marxists to argue that the Media (especially the news) are controlled by a sinister group of billionaires who brainwash everyone through **ideology**. This underestimates the independence of many journalists, teachers and bosses as well as the ability of ordinary people to think for themselves and work out what's true. *However* Post-Marxism reinterprets this as discourses that give privileges to hegemonic groups rather than an actual conspiracy.

Marxists assume class is homogenous: *Homogenous* means 'all the same' and traditional Marxists think that all working class people share the same relationship to labour and power. *However*, **Intersectionality** focuses on oppressed Identities intersecting, distinguishing between working class people who are elderly or female.

Marxism offers no solutions: You don't have to be a Marxist to spot the Capitalism has flaws! Marxists argue that Capitalism is intrinsically rotten and destructive and it needs to be replaced rather than reformed. But replaced with what? Marxism can be accused of criticising Capitalism without offering a coherent alternative. *However*, the **Social Justice** movement has projects to improve equity for marginalised and disadvantaged groups.

Feminism

Feminism ignores biology: Feminists insist that gender is **socially constructed,** and it certainly is up to a point. However, Psychology reveals lots of biological differences in brain structure, hormones and genes between the sexes and it's unlikely that *none* of this makes *any* difference to social behaviour. *However*, Gender Identity theory (popular with 3rd & 4th Wave Feminists) suggests that sex is *not* based on biology at all and **Judith Butler** argues Gender is **performative** (something you do, not something you are).

Feminism ignores progress: In the last century women have won the vote, the right to be educated at university and manage their own affairs. In Britain, the Sexual Discrimination Act (1975) has outlawed sexual discrimination. Feminism can be accused of downplaying this progress and exaggerating the scale of injustice. *However*, **misogynist Trolls** and murderous **Incels** show that there is still violent hatred towards women.

Feminists assume gender is homogenous: As with Marxists and social class, traditional Feminists are accused of treating all women as if they experienced the same oppression – which in practice means assuming that the difficulties of White women are typical for all women. *However*, **3ʳᵈ & 4ᵗʰ Wave Feminism** incorporates **Intersectionality** which distinguishes between different feminine Identities (e.g. young and elderly women).

Feminists ignore the oppression of men: Feminists sometimes seem to assume that Masculinity is homogenous and all men are complicit in the Patriarchy, but men are much more likely than women to die by violence, to be victims of crime and to work in dangerous conditions. *However*, online sexual abuse, harassment and rape threats are disproportionately aimed at women, not men.

Postmodernism

Postmodernism ignores continuing modernity: The Internet has made huge changes to our lives, along with technology like mobile phones and satellite TV. However, life for many people continues as it did in the 1960s, '70s and '80s: they live in nuclear families, work in factories or offices, take part in religious worship and live in different social classes. Only a minority of people – and perhaps, only in a few big cities – enjoys the unusual, ever-changing, online lifestyles that Postmodernism claims are typical. This is **Giddens'** argument for **Late Modernity**.

Postmodernists reject objective truth: By rejecting **meta-narratives**, Postmodernism rejects objective truth. Nothing is absolutely and provably true, it can only ever be subjective truth (true-for-you or true-as-you-see-it). But how can social problems be solved unless we agree they objectively *are* problems? Why should sociological research be taken seriously if it's only a point of view? How can we tell good points of view from wild conspiracy theories and 'fake news'?

Postmodernism only applies to some topics: Postmodernism is great for explaining shifts in style and fashion, personal Identity, consumer choice and lifestyles, especially online lifestyles. It's less good for tackling the harder topics of poverty, discrimination and violence. It **also lacks political solutions** for tackling these things. *However*, there is now **Applied Postmodernism** found in 3ʳᵈ & 4ᵗʰ Wave Feminism or Post-Marxism which is more politically active (e.g. the **Social Justice** movement).

EXAM PRACTICE: SECTION A

The OCR exam has three questions in **Paper 3 Section A**:

Source A	Source B
The 2020-21 Coronavirus Pandemic forced many of us to move to online networking. We worked from home, using email and videoconferencing. We studied from home, completing assignments on websites. We socialised in virtual communities and reached out to loved ones through cyberspace. Unable to travel or fly, business meeting moved online and virtual travel guides showed off foreign destinations to home-bound tourists. While the world was locked down, the Internet showed us we were really more connected than ever.	The problem with the Internet is that it offers more to the haves than the have-nots. If you're already well-off and educated, you can take full advantage of the Internet to study, learn new skills, make valuable contacts and find good jobs. The poorest people can't afford powerful smart phones or tablets. Even when they get them, they lack the ability to make full use of them – and online gambling and shopping sites are always there to take their money. Online, we're more unequal than ever.

1. With references to the Source[s], define what sociologists mean by a networked global society. **[9 marks: 5 AO1 + 4 AO2]**

*Make two sociological points about global networks, one based on Source A and one on Source B. You should quote from the source. It's not vital to refer to named sociologists but you should definitely use some sociological terminology. Then offer examples of global networks and make sure each example has an explanation of **why** it is a global network. For example, "Using a Social Media site like Goodwall to find out about jobs and internships in other countries."*

2. With references to the Source[s], to what extent does a networked global society improve people's social capital? **[10 marks: 4 AO1 + 2 AO2 + 4 AO3]**

Write a paragraph about source A then another about source B. Sum up what's in the source and explain what named sociologists would say about it. Then finish off with a brief evaluation of each view (p65). Make sure you conclude by answering the question (it does improve social capital or it doesn't or perhaps it only improves it for some people but not others).

3. Evaluate the view that digital forms of communication have contributed to conflict in the world. **[16 marks: 4 AO1 + 4 AO2 + 8 AO3]**

Write three paragraphs. Each paragraph should introduce a sociological idea with some illustration from the real world. Each paragraph should finish off with developed evaluation (see p69 for this). For example, you could write about the Culture Wars, online hate groups and terrorists organising themselves online. Don't forget to answer the question: does the Internet lead to more conflict or not?

KEY RESEARCH

The 24 studies here cover all the topics that arise in this Section of the exam and they will prove just as useful in other sections too. Start learning them. For each study, I include the key terms, a Perspective (if relevant) and the particular topics it is linked to.

Boyle (2007): demand-led vs supply-led New Media; **Interactionist**; media convergence, p32

Burgess (2020): digital divide, digital skills, digital exclusion; impact on inequality, networked global society, p58

Butler (1990): *Gender Trouble*, performative gender, gendered reality, Queer Theory; **Feminist**; impact on identity & inequality, p44

Castells (2000): *The Information Age*, informational Capitalism, the Information Age; **Neo-Marxism**; networked global society, impact on inequality, p31

Cornford & Robins (1999): evolutionary vs revolutionary New Media; **Marxism**; digital revolution, media convergence, impact on inequality, conflict & change, p28

Curran & Seaton (1991): patterns of ownership, oligarchy; **Marxist**; social media, social capital, impact on equality, cultural homogeneity, conflict & change, p39

Duffy (2021): traditionalists, progressives, moderates & disengaged, culture wars; conflict & change, impact on inequality, p46

Foucault (1966): discourses, regimes of truth, deconstruction, problematising; **Postmodernist**; impact on identity & inequality, p40

Friedman (1999): *Lexus & the Olive* Tree, Golden Arches Theory of conflict prevention; **Functionalist**; cultural homogenisation, p48

Giddens (1999): *Runaway World*, Late Modernity, detraditionalization, cosmopolitanism, manufactured risk; **Interactionist**; defining Globalisation, cultural defence, impact on Identities, p7, p9

Goodhart (2017): *The Road to Somewhere*, Somewheres vs Anywheres; **Functionalism**; defining Globalisation, impact on Identity, conflict & change, p15

Haraway (1985): *A Cyborg Manifesto*, cyborgs; **Feminism**; impact on identity & inequality, conflict & change, p54

Hu & Qian (2021): online loneliness; impact on inequality & relationships, p60

Laclau & Mouffe (1985): *Hegemony & Socialist Strategy*, hegemony, antagonism; **Post-Marxist**; impact on inequality, conflict & change, p42

McLuhan (1964): global village, the medium is the message; **Interactionist**; global village, impact on identity & relationships, cultural homogeneity; p29

Miller (2011): *Tales From Facebook*; **Interactionist**; social media, virtual community, impact on relationships, p62

Moloney & Love (2018): Virtual Manhood Acts (VMA), online sexual harassment, gendertrolling, e-bile, disciplinary rhetoric; **Interactionist**; impact on inequality & identity, p59

Noveck et al. (2021): online community-building; **Weberian**; social media, virtual communities, impact on relationships, p35

Page (2019): *Perennials: the future of ageing*, perennials, nostalgia; **Weberian**; impact on identity, p56

Putnam (2000): *Bowling Alone*, social capital; **Functionalism**; social capital, p21

Ritzer (1993): *The McDonaldization of Society*, McDonaldisation, efficiency, calculability, predictability, control; **Weberian**; glocalisation, 50

Robinson (2004): transnational state, transnational bourgeoisie; **Marxist**; defining Globalisation, impact on inequality, conflict & change, p12

Ronson (2015): *So You've Been Publicly Shamed*, shaming; **Interactionist**; social media, virtual communities, impact on relationships, p34

Tufecki (2017): *Twitter & Tear Gas*, decentralised online movements, tactical freezes; **Post-Marxism**; impact on identity & equality, conflict & change, p52

FURTHER RESEARCH

These studies are less central to any argument. Some of them just reference a useful piece of terminology. Others offer criticism of a Key Study or are the original research that a Key Study is criticising.

Bates (2012): *Everyday Sexism Project*, p24

Baudrillard (1970): hyper-reality, simulacrum, p22

Bauman (2013): postmodern uncertainty, p40, 61

Bindel (2017): against sex-positivity, Gender Critical, p25

Bor & Peterson (2021): Mismatch Theory explains online conflict, p35

Bourdieu (1984): social reproduction not meritocracy, p56

Case (2007): supports **Haraway (1985)**, p54

Crenshaw (1991): intersectionality; p24

Duffy & Hewlett (2021): US culture wars exported to the UK, p46

Geraci et al. (2018): supports **Putnam (2000)**, p21

Livingstone (2018): transphobia on Mumsnet, p53

Lyotard (1979): death of meta-narratives, p22, 40

McIntosh (1988): white privilege, p51

Morozov (2011): slacktivism, p52

Postman (1994): *The Disappearance of Childhood*, p54

Turkle (2011): *Alone Together*, p61

Yee (2006): survey of relationships on *World of Warcraft*, p35

GLOSSARY

Capitalism: an economic system that promotes the private ownership of property, the pursuit of profit and the concentration of wealth in the hands of a minority of people; the opposite is Communism, which abolishes private property to make everyone economically equal

Cultural defence: ways that members of a culture can resist **homogenisation** due to **globalisation**; may lead to **glocalisation**

Culture: the set of norms and values passed on by one generation to the next, including a version of history and traditional institutions that make up a way of life; cultures vary from one society to another and change (slowly) over time

Deconstruction: technique to expose the hidden values in **discourse** and weaken the power encoded in language, usually by exposing bias, questioning ordinary meanings and playing around with possible meanings.

Digital Divide: the separation of people into those who can and those who cannot take full advantage of the Internet

Digital Forms of Communication (DFOC): ways of interacting with other people through the Internet, such as sending or receiving text messages or emails or posting on websites

Digital Revolution: transformation in communications technology brought on by the invention of computers

Discourse: a way of using language that is coded with assumptions about power and privilege; using this language reinforces inequality in society but **deconstructing** it can empower oppressed or marginalised groups

Feminism: a sociological Perspective that identified conflict between the sexes; believes in a Patriarchy which subordinates women and maintains male power through coercion and violence

Functionalism: a sociological Perspective that promotes consensus around shared values; believes in a biological basis for human social behaviour and a March of Progress that has produced liberal democratic nations as the most successful way of living

Gender role: the social expectations that go with gender; masculinity is often linked with aggression, ambition, intelligence and high status; femininity is often linked with passivity, emotion and subordinate status; gender roles lead to the expectation of different career choices for men and women and different expectations about responsibilities in the home

Gender: the norms and values linked to biological sex; males are often expected to behave in a masculine way and females in a feminine way: male/female are sexes but masculine/feminine are genders

Globalisation: a process going on that makes different parts of the world more interconnected through travel, global **Capitalism** and the **Mass Media**; results in the spread of Global Culture and Hybrid Culture but is sometimes resisted

Glocalisation: a process combining the influence of **Globalisation** with local culture; may be a result of cultural defence creating a Hybrid Culture or a strategy by global Capitalism to make its products more attractive

Hegemony: the dominance of one group and their culture in society; hegemonic culture is the version of culture that commands the most respect; hegemonic culture might be the culture of the majority of people but it is more often the culture of a wealthy and influential elite

Heteronormative: privileging heterosexual people, stigmatising gays, lesbians and gender non-conformist or non-binary people

Homogenisation: a process of removing differences and distinctions so that everyone becomes similar; the opposite is heterogenisation

Ideology: a set of ideas and values that influence how people interpret society; ideology is usually promoted by the **hegemonic** culture hides and justifies things which go against that culture; for example, a racist ideology might make people ignore racism or (if they can't ignore it) view racism as justified

Interactionism: a sociological Perspective that adopts a micro (small scale) approach; believes in understand individual motives and perceptions

Intersectionality: approach to Sociology which focuses on how different identities combine to create privilege or oppression

Marxism: a sociological Perspective that identifies conflict between social classes; believes in a **ruling class** exploiting a **working class**, both through violet force and **ruling class ideology**

Mass Media: technological forms of communication that can reach millions (or billions of people); traditionally radio, TV, film and print but now including the digital media, such as websites, social media, text messaging and mobile phones

Materialism: traditional approach to **Marxism** and **2nd Wave Feminism** which focuses on identifying and challenging the inequality in people's material circumstances (as opposed to the language being used to describe them)

Meritocracy: the opposite of **Social Reproduction**; the idea that individuals can gain wealth and privilege through hard work and talent

Multiculturalism: the idea that society can and should include people from different cultures without demanding that they abandon their native culture in order to assimilate

Neo-Marxism: several new interpretations of **Marxism** that emerged in the 1970s and became mainstream in the 1990s, incorporating elements of **Interactionism** and later **Postmodernism** to traditional Marxist thought (*c.f.* **Post-Marxism**).

New Media: platforms based around **digital forms of communication** that offer more interactivity and choice that the traditional media (e.g. satellite TV, digital radio, streaming music or videos)

New Right: a sociological Perspective not covered in this book that proposes we are experience social collapse brought on by a welfare culture that rewards worklessness and deviance

Patriarchy: The way society is structured around the interests of males, giving status to masculine behaviour and values and systematically subordinating women; masculine **hegemony** in society

Post-Marxism: development of **Neo-Marxism** that incorporates **Postmodern** ideas about **discourse** and **deconstruction**

Postmodernism: a sociological Perspective that proposes we are living in a new phase of social development, characterised by media images, diversity, choice and fragmentation

Privilege: the advantages a person has, perhaps without realising it, because they belong to high-status groups or have Identities that are respected in society

Queer Theory: development of 3rd Wave Feminism that views society as dominated by **heteronormative discourses** that privilege straight men and which need to be 'queered' to show up their falseness

Ruling class: A **hegemonic** group in society that controls the wealth and power, supported by an ideology that either hides or justifies their influence

Ruling class ideology: a set of beliefs promoted by the ruling class to preserve their power over the working class; ideology hides the injustice in society and justifies it when it cannot hide it

Social capital: social connections (friends, family, followers, etc) which give you influence and power in society

Social class: a system for separating people based on their economic position (wealth, income, status); originally a split between the **ruling class** and **working class**, but later admitting of a middle class in between and now many more classes

Socialisation: The process of acquiring norms and values due to upbringing (primary socialisation) and education/experience (secondary socialisation)

Social reproduction: the opposite of **Meritocracy**; the idea that social divisions are reproduced each generation despite the education people receive

Values: powerful ideas shared by people in a culture about what is right and desirable and what is shameful or wrong; often expressed in behaviour as **norms**

Western culture: the culture of the UK, European countries, North America and Australia, that emerged out of the shared experience of Christianity, the Industrial Revolution and the development of democracy; an important part of **Global Culture**; responsible for developing Capitalism

ABOUT THE AUTHOR

Jonathan Rowe is a teacher of Religious Studies, Psychology and Sociology at Spalding Grammar School and he creates and maintains **www.psychologywizard.net** and the **www.philosophydungeon.weebly.com** site for Edexcel A-Level Religious Studies. He has worked as an examiner for various Exam Boards but is not affiliated with OCR. This series of books grew out of the resources he created for his students. Jonathan also writes novels and creates resources for his hobby of fantasy wargaming. He likes warm beer and smooth jazz.

Jonathan has created the **Sociology Robot** YouTube channel with video lectures supporting the material in this Study Guide.

Printed in Great Britain
by Amazon

82133996R00045